ENCOUNTERS *with* CHRIST

Becoming Fishers of Men

JASON KING

LUCIDBOOKS

Encounters with Christ: Becoming Fishers of Men

Published by Lucid Books in Houston, TX
www.LucidBooks.com

ISBN: 978-1-63296-995-8 (Paperback)
ISBN: 978-1-63296-997-2 (Hardback)
eISBN: 978-1-63296-999-6

Special Sales: Most Lucid Books titles are available in special quantity discounts. Custom imprinting or excerpting can also be done to fit special needs. Contact Lucid Books at Info@LucidBooks.com

To those who walked the streets with me in prayer—
listening, loving, and trusting God to work in unseen ways.
This book was shaped by those steps of obedience.

Then He said to them, "Follow Me,
and I will make you fishers of men."
—Matt. 4:19

Training believers to reach the world—
one encounter at a time

CONTENTS

Preface

From the time I came to faith in Christ, evangelism became one of the deepest burdens of my heart. I wanted to understand how to share my faith faithfully and lovingly, so I read books, attended trainings, and learned various methods. The techniques were helpful, but I often felt disconnected from the real conversations I was having with people. As I spent more time in the Gospels, I began to see that Jesus' approach to evangelism looked very different from much of what we emphasize today. His encounters were personal and thoughtful. He listened, asked questions, exposed the heart, and spoke truth with perfect wisdom and compassion.

Several years ago, I began prayer-walking in the heart of Anniston, Alabama—often with my wife and a few close friends. It wasn't the safest place to be, but it was exactly where we sensed the Lord leading us. On those streets we met people from every background imaginable, and those conversations shaped me more than any formal training ever had. It was there on quiet Saturday mornings that I learned to slow down, pay attention, and truly listen. I learned to hear people's stories, discern their struggles, and meet them right where they were. Those mornings remain among the most formative moments of my life.

This book grew out of that journey. As I continued studying the encounters Jesus had with people—Nicodemus, the Samaritan woman, the crowds, the skeptics, the desperate, and the indifferent—I began to notice patterns. Jesus never used the same approach twice. He met each person with exactly what they needed. He understood motives, fears, false confidence, confusion, and deep longing. And He consistently addressed the heart, not just the mind. Over time, I realized that the church as a whole could benefit from returning to Jesus' way of engaging people with the gospel.

My prayer is that this book helps believers grow in discernment, develop a deeper dependence on the Holy Spirit, and gain confidence to speak about Christ in everyday conversations. I hope these familiar stories open your eyes to the wisdom and compassion of Jesus, showing not only what He said but how He approached each person. Evangelism is not merely about knowing what to say; it is about walking with God, loving people well, and trusting Him to lead each conversation in His perfect timing.

—Jason King

Introduction

REDISCOVERING THE MASTER'S WAY

It all began on the shores of Galilee. Fishermen were mending their nets after a long, fruitless night with tired hands, worn faces, and boats that told the story of failure. Then Jesus stepped into one of those boats, and everything changed. When He finished teaching, He turned to Peter and issued a command that made no sense to a weary fisherman: "Launch out into the deep and let down your nets for a catch" (Luke 5:4). What happened next stunned them all. The nets grew heavy, the boat shifted under the weight, and Peter fell to his knees in awe.

That moment was more than a miracle of fish. It was the beginning of a calling. Jesus wasn't handing Peter a formula or a script. He was inviting him into a partnership: "Follow Me, and I will make you fishers of men" (Matt. 4:19). Evangelism, from the very first moment, was not a technique to master; it was a relationship to enter, a walk of obedience powered by the presence of Christ Himself. The same invitation goes out to every believer today—to step into deeper waters, trust His Word, and join Him in His rescue mission for souls.

For many, evangelism has become a source of anxiety. We've been handed outlines and presentations—helpful tools in their place—but somewhere along the way, we lost the art of listening and discerning. We remember our points yet often forget the people standing in front of us.

Jesus never took that approach. Instead of using a one-size-fits-all method, He met people where they were, listened with compassion, asked questions that probed the heart, and spoke truth with grace. If you study His conversations, you'll notice that no two are alike. He told Nicodemus about the new birth and the Samaritan woman about living water. He held up the law to the rich young ruler and extended grace to the adulterous woman. He spoke gently to some and firmly to others, yet His purpose never changed: to lead people from darkness to light. To Jesus, evangelism was never a presentation. It was an encounter.

Today, many of us long to experience that same clarity and effectiveness but feel unsure where to begin. We know the gospel is powerful. We know we are called to share it. Yet evangelism often feels intimidating, awkward, and unpredictable. Conversations rarely follow the outlines we've practiced. We sometimes walk away wondering if we said too much, too little, or the wrong thing altogether. And for some, evangelism becomes something reserved for pastors, extroverts, or people with a "gift for it."

But Jesus never limited His call to a select few. He invited ordinary people—fishermen, tax collectors, and everyday believers—to join Him in His mission. The power to reach people does not come from our personality, confidence, or ability. It comes from the Holy Spirit working through the Word of God as we walk in obedience to Christ. Evangelism is not something we perform for God but something God does through us as we learn to abide in Him.

This book is an invitation to rediscover the Master's way of reaching people. We begin by laying the foundations of biblical evangelism—the call to cast the net, the role of the Spirit, and the power of the Word. From there, we step into Scripture's living encounters. Each story reveals a different kind of heart: the religious, the broken, the self-righteous, the self-justifying, the guilty, the bound, the doubting, and the seeking. As we walk beside Jesus in these moments, we learn not only what He said but why He said it. His discernment becomes our pattern. His compassion shapes our approach. His truth guides our conversations.

My hope is that this book equips you, not with a script to memorize but with eyes to see, ears to hear, and a heart willing to be led by the Spirit. Evangelism is not about being impressive or persuasive. It is about walking closely with Jesus, listening with compassion, speaking with grace, and trusting that God alone brings the increase.

The same Savior who stepped into Peter's boat still steps

into the lives of ordinary believers today. The waters may feel deep. The task may feel overwhelming. But His Word still stands: "Launch out into the deep and let down your nets." And He is still in the boat.

As you journey through these pages, may you rediscover the joy, the confidence, and the calling of becoming a fisher of men—following the Master one encounter at a time.

PART 1

FOUNDATIONS FOR EVANGELISM

Preparing the
Heart and Mind for the Mission

Chapter 1

CASTING THE NET

Answering the Call to Evangelism

Main Passage: Luke 5:1–11

Key Verse: *Launch out into the deep and let down your nets for a catch.* —Luke 5:4

When Jesus Calls You

Jesus came to the shores of Galilee where fishermen were mending their nets and preparing for another day's work. Peter, Andrew, James, and John were ordinary men doing ordinary things. There was nothing remarkable about the moment, yet it was there that the call to change the world began.

Hours of labor had produced nothing—no catch, no income, only exhaustion. The rhythm of casting and drawing had become an echo of futility. Then Jesus arrived. He did not bring new equipment or a better technique; He brought

His presence. Stepping into Peter's boat, He asked him to push out a little from the land. It was a simple request but deeply personal. Before Jesus called Peter to follow Him, He first entered Peter's ordinary life. Evangelism does not begin with grand strategy or exceptional skill. It begins when Jesus steps into the familiar spaces of our everyday routines.

After Jesus finished teaching, He gave Peter a personal command: "Launch out into the deep and let down your nets for a catch" (v. 4). Peter hesitated. He had already fished all night and caught nothing. He was exhausted, and his expertise told him this made no sense. But he said, "Nevertheless at Your word I will let down the net" (v. 5). It was reluctant faith, but it was faith, nonetheless. Moments later, the still water boiled with life. The nets strained, and the boats filled to the point of sinking. Overwhelmed, Peter fell to his knees and confessed, "Depart from me, for I am a sinful man, O Lord!" (v. 8). Yet Jesus did not depart. He called out, "Do not be afraid. From now on you will catch men" (v. 10).

This scene is more than a miracle of fish. It is the unveiling of Christ's method for reaching the world. Jesus was showing Peter that the obedience that filled the nets would one day bring people into the kingdom. Every element—His presence, His command, the partnership, Peter's humility, and the new purpose—foreshadows the Great Commission. Here on Galilee's shore, the pattern of evangelism is born.

When Jesus Steps into Your Boat

Jesus began His ministry not in synagogues or temples but among ordinary people in ordinary places. He stepped into a fishing boat—into Peter's workplace, his routine, his familiar world. That is where the call to follow Christ begins for all of us: where we live, work, and walk through the rhythms of life.

Jesus does not wait for us to be prepared, polished, or spiritually confident. Peter did not invite Jesus into his boat; Jesus entered by His own initiative. Evangelism doesn't begin with our skill or boldness; it begins with Christ's presence. The work He calls us to depends not on our strength but on His nearness. Before Peter ever cast a net, he simply sat with Jesus in the boat. This moment pointed to a greater truth: "Then He appointed twelve, that they might be with Him and that He might send them out to preach" (Mark 3:14).

This is where evangelism is often misunderstood. Before we are called to go *for* Him, we are called to be *with* Him. Scripture teaches that fruit comes from abiding, not striving (John 15:5).

Peter's boat represented his identity, security, and rhythm of life. When Jesus stepped into it, the center of Peter's life was being reordered. Jesus does not remain a silent passenger in the background. He becomes the One who directs where the boat goes and where the nets are cast.

When Jesus steps into our lives, He does not simply bless

our plans; He redirects them. His call is not an invitation to fit Him into an already full life but to let Him define its direction and purpose. Evangelism is not something we perform for Christ but something that flows from walking with Him. We speak of Him because we have been with Him. And as we learn to abide in His presence, He leads us into deeper waters where faith becomes obedience and obedience becomes fruit.

Deeper Waters, Greater Faith

When Jesus finished teaching, He turned His attention to Peter. The lesson was no longer for the crowd. It was for the man in the boat. "Launch out into the deep" (v. 4). This command moved Peter from the familiar shallows into the unknown waters of trust.

The deep represents the place of risk and faith, the place beyond our comfort zone. Jesus' instruction didn't make sense to Peter. Everything in him said, "This won't work." Yet he replied, "Nevertheless at Your word." This is where faith begins: not when circumstances make sense but when the word of Christ outweighs our own understanding. Jesus leads us into places where our effort cannot produce results, so we learn that fruitfulness belongs to Him. The deep waters are where our confidence in ourselves ends and our dependence on Him begins.

Evangelism will always feel like deep water. It requires trusting Christ beyond our comfort and competence. We don't speak because we feel bold. We speak because He has spoken. We don't share because we are persuasive. We share because He is present. When Peter obeyed, the nets began to break and the boats began to sink under the weight of the catch. The results belonged to Jesus, not Peter. Peter cast the net; Jesus filled it.

This is the rhythm of evangelism:

We obey – He draws.
We speak – He saves.
We go – He works.

Paul captured the same truth: "I planted, Apollos watered, but God gave the increase" (1 Cor. 3:6).

You're Not Meant to Fish Alone

God is the One who gives the increase. Our part is to labor together in faithfulness, just as Paul planted and Apollos watered. The pattern is the same on the Sea of Galilee. When the nets began to fill, Peter could not bring in the catch alone. He signaled for his partners to come and help because the work was too great for one set of hands.

Evangelism was never designed to be carried out in isolation. It is shared work. Jesus calls us into the mission together so the burden is lighter, the encouragement stronger, and the joy multiplied. The nets are steadier when more hands hold them.

When Jesus later sent out His disciples, He sent them

two by two (Luke 10:1). The early church followed this pattern: Paul and Barnabas, Paul and Silas, Timothy and Luke, Aquila and Priscilla. Evangelism has always moved forward through partnership.

Sharing Christ can feel daunting when we imagine ourselves doing it alone. We need others to pray with us, encourage us, go with us, and help carry the weight of the work. Just as the nets required more than one fisherman, the mission requires the fellowship of believers.

Find someone to pray with. Walk together. Cast the net together. The joy of the catch and the strain of the work were always meant to be shared.

When Holiness Meets a Broken Heart

When Peter saw the overwhelming catch, he realized this was no ordinary teacher in his boat. The power and purity of Christ's presence brought his own condition into sharp focus. He fell to his knees and said, "Depart from me, for I am a sinful man, O Lord!" (v. 8).

This is the natural response when the holiness of Christ meets the honesty of a human heart. The light of Jesus does not expose us to shame us but to make us see our need. Peter was not being pushed away from grace; he was being drawn toward it. Conviction is not God rejecting us; it is God awakening us.

Jesus did not rebuke Peter for his confession. He did not turn away. Instead, He spoke the words Peter most needed:

"Do not be afraid" (v. 10). The holiness of Christ did not crush Peter. It restored him. Grace does not deny sin. It meets us in it and leads us out.

Evangelism begins here—not with superiority, performance, or polished language but with a heart humbled by grace. We cannot truly tell others about Jesus until we ourselves have been undone and remade by His presence. The one who knows they have been forgiven much is the one who will speak much of Christ.

From the Shore to the World

After the boats reached the shore, Peter, Andrew, James, and John left everything to follow Jesus (v. 11). The miracle was not the goal; the call was. Jesus had shown them who He was, and now He was showing them what their lives were meant for. They were no longer defined by nets and fish but by a mission that would reach the world.

The call of Christ always moves us outward. The grace that meets us in our boat is the same grace that sends us into the lives of others. But Jesus does not send us alone. The One who says, "Follow Me" is the same One who promises, "I am with you always." He does not call us to accomplish the impossible. He calls us to walk with Him as He accomplishes His work through us.

Evangelism is not reserved for the bold, the eloquent, or the theologically trained. It is the overflow of a heart changed by Christ. We speak because we have been reached. We invite because we have been welcomed. We call others because He first called us.

From the shore of Galilee, the world was changed through ordinary people who followed an extraordinary Savior. And the same Savior continues His work today through tax-preparers, mechanics, teachers, mothers, students, pastors, neighbors, and friends. You do not have to change the world. You do not have to save anyone. You do not have to produce results. You simply follow. You cast. You trust. The increase is His.

Key Verses to Remember

Luke 5:5 – *Nevertheless at Your word I will let down the net.*

- Obedience begins when Christ's word outweighs our understanding.

Mark 3:14 – *Then He appointed twelve, that they might be with Him and that He might send them out to preach.*

- Evangelism flows from being with Jesus before speaking for Him.

John 15:5 – *I am the vine, you* are *the branches. He who abides in Me, and I in him, bears much fruit; for without Me you can do nothing.*

- True fruit comes from abiding in Christ, not from our effort.

Luke 10:1 – *After these things, the Lord appointed seventy others also, and sent them two by two.*

- The mission is shared; we go together.

1 Corinthians 3:6 – *I planted, Apollos watered, but God gave the increase.*

- We labor faithfully; God alone produces the results.

Principles for Today

- Jesus initiates the work of evangelism.
- We follow because He first entered our lives and called us to Himself.
- Evangelism flows from abiding, not striving.
- Our witness is the overflow of being with Jesus, not performing for Him.
- Obedience matters more than expertise.
- We cast the net in faith and trust God to give the increase.
- The mission is shared, not solo.
- We labor together in fellowship, prayer, and encouragement.
- Grace forms the heart of a true witness.
- Humbled hearts speak of Christ with compassion and sincerity.

- Christ sends us, but He goes with us.
- The One who calls us to follow also promises His presence in the work.

Questions for Reflection and Practice

1. Where has Jesus "stepped into your boat"—your ordinary routines—recently?
2. What is one "deep water" step of obedience the Lord may be calling you to take?
3. Who could you partner with in prayer and encouragement as you share Christ?

Closing Thoughts

Jesus shows us that evangelism begins with simple obedience—casting the net even when the results seem uncertain. Every encounter carries the potential for someone to respond to the truth, and God uses our willingness more than our ability. This chapter reminds us that sharing the gospel is not about creating outcomes but offering opportunities. As you step into conversations, trust that God prepares hearts long before you speak. May you move forward with courage, knowing that faithful sowing often leads to eternal harvests in ways you may never see until heaven.

Chapter 2

The Spirit's Work

Partnering with God in Evangelism

Main Passage: John 16:7–11

Key Verse: *It is to your advantage that I go away; for if I do not go away, the Helper will not come to you; but if I depart, I will send Him to you.* —John 16:7

Why It Was Better for Jesus to Leave

The disciples had left everything to follow Jesus, so His words must have stunned them: "It is to your advantage that I go away" (v. 7). How could losing Jesus possibly be an advantage? Their Teacher, their Miracle Worker, their Friend—the One who walked on water and stilled storms—was speaking of His departure as if it were progress. Yet Jesus was preparing them for something greater than His presence beside them: the Spirit's presence within them.

The coming of the Holy Spirit would not be a downgrade but an expansion of Christ's ministry. He would take the same divine presence that filled Christ's earthly life and multiply it through His followers. What had once been limited to one Man in one place would now fill every believer in every nation.

Jesus called Him the "Helper"—the *Paraklētos,* the One who comes alongside to comfort, guide, convict, and empower. The Spirit is not a passive presence but the active power of God working in the hearts of His people. The mission of making disciples would not rest on human boldness or persuasive skill but on divine strength.

This is why Jesus could say, without exaggeration, that the Spirit's presence was to their advantage. The Spirit does not merely encourage the believer; He enables the impossible. The same Spirit who hovered over the waters at creation now moves in the hearts of men and women to bring new life. Every true work of evangelism begins not with our effort but with His power.

The Spirit Who Works as We Speak

When we speak the gospel, we are never speaking alone. The Holy Spirit is at work in unseen ways—opening eyes, softening hearts, exposing need, and drawing people to Christ. Jesus said the Spirit would "convict the world of sin, and of righteousness, and of judgment" (v. 8). That work is His, not ours.

This truth should reshape how we see evangelism. We are not trying to persuade someone into the kingdom by the force of our words. We are bearing witness to Christ while the Spirit works in the depths of the heart. Even when our words feel weak or imperfect, the Spirit uses them with power.

This is why no conversation about Christ is ever wasted. A seed planted in casual conversation, a scripture shared in passing, a testimony offered in humility—each one becomes a tool in the Spirit's hands. We speak the truth; He makes it living. The Spirit is not the assistant to our witness; we are the assistants to His. We cast the net; He moves the fish.

This frees us from pressure and fear. We are not responsible for producing spiritual results. We are responsible to be faithful, not forceful. If someone responds, we rejoice. If they do not, we trust that the Spirit is still working beyond what we can see. Evangelism, then, is not a performance to master. It is a partnership to embrace. We speak, He works. He is the invisible Partner in every gospel conversation, the unseen Hand pressing truth upon the conscience.

How the Spirit Awakens the Heart

The first evidence of the Spirit's work in a person's life is often awareness, a quiet sense that something is missing, broken, or unresolved. The same message that may sound ordinary to one person can suddenly feel personal, weighty, and impossible to ignore to another. This is the heart beginning to awaken.

Jesus described this as being drawn by the Father (John 6:44). The Spirit gently brings a person to recognize the emptiness of life apart from God, the weight of sin, and the need for forgiveness. This awakening is not something we create but something God does. We cannot manufacture conviction, pressure someone into repentance, or talk them into salvation. Only the Spirit can reveal the true condition of the heart.

And when He does, the person may not immediately respond with repentance. Sometimes there is resistance. Sometimes questions surface. Sometimes the heart wrestles. But the wrestling itself is a sign of God's mercy. Conviction is not the judgment of God; it is the invitation of God. It is the gracious work of the Spirit saying, "There is more. Come."

Our role in this moment is not to rush, push, or force. It is to walk gently, listen, and speak truth with patience and compassion. We trust that the Spirit is moving even when we cannot see what is happening beneath the surface. The net is in the water. The heart is stirring. God is working.

Spirit-Given Power, Not Self-Made Pressure

We often hesitate to share Christ because we feel inadequate. We think we need more confidence, more knowledge, or the perfect words. But the power for evangelism does not come from our personality or ability. It comes from the Spirit who lives in us. Jesus did not say, "You will be My witnesses when you feel ready." He said, "You shall receive power when the Holy Spirit has come upon you" (Acts 1:8). The power comes first; the witness flows from it.

Jesus told His disciples to wait for the Spirit because He had not yet been given. But now, every believer has received the Spirit (Rom. 8:9). We are not waiting for power; we are walking in the presence of the One who has already been given.

The boldness we long for often comes in the moment we obey. When we step forward, however small the step may be, the Holy Spirit supplies what we lack. The words come that we feared we could not say. The peace we did not feel arrives. The strength we thought we lacked is given. We do not speak because we feel strong. We speak because He is with us.

The Spirit who empowered the disciples is the same Spirit who lives in you today. He does not need your strength—only your willingness. Our role is to trust, abide, and open our mouths when the moment comes. The rest belongs to Him. Evangelism is not pressure but dependence. It is not self-confidence but Spirit-confidence. It is not striving but abiding. When we depend on Him, our words carry eternal weight because His Spirit breathes life through them.

The Spirit's Purpose: To Glorify Christ

Jesus described the Spirit's ultimate purpose in John 16:14: "He will glorify Me." The aim of every conversation, every seed planted, and every testimony shared is that Jesus would be seen for who He truly is. We do not draw attention to ourselves. We do not point others to our own righteousness, wisdom, or strength. The Spirit leads both the witness and the hearer to look to Christ.

This frees us from self-consciousness, from fear of failure, and from pressure to convince or perform. If the purpose of evangelism were to prove ourselves, the weight would be unbearable. But the purpose is to make Christ known, and He is worthy to be spoken of. The Spirit fills our hearts with worship so our words flow from love, not burden.

When we speak of Christ, we do so with quiet confidence that He is near. The Spirit goes before us, works in us, and continues long after the conversation ends. Our role is not to produce faith but to faithfully bear witness to the One who saved us. We open our mouths, and the Spirit honors Christ through our words.

The same God who empowered the first disciples empowers us. The same Spirit who awakened our hearts continues to awaken others. And the same Christ who called us calls us still: "Follow Me." All glory to Christ, the One we proclaim.

Key Verses to Remember

John 14:16–17 – *He will give you another Helper, that He may abide with you forever . . . for He dwells with you and will be in you.*

- The Spirit is not merely near us; He lives within us.

John 16:8 – *And when He has come, He will convict the world of sin, and of righteousness, and of judgment.*

- Conviction is the Spirit's work, not ours.

Acts 1:8 – *But you shall receive power when the Holy Spirit has come upon you; and you shall be witnesses to Me.*

- The Spirit empowers our witness.

1 Corinthians 2:4–5 – *My speech and my preaching* were *not with persuasive words of human wisdom, but in demonstration of the Spirit and of power.*

- The effectiveness of the gospel rests on the Spirit, not our eloquence.

Romans 8:26 – *Likewise the Spirit also helps in our weaknesses.*

- We witness from dependence, not perfection or confidence.

Principles for Today

- The Spirit is the believer's Helper.
- We do not share Christ alone; He is present in every conversation.
- The Spirit works while we speak.
- We bear witness, but He awakens the heart.
- Conviction is a work of grace.

- When someone begins to feel their need, God is already drawing them.
- Boldness grows in obedience.
- Strength is supplied in the step of faith, not before it.
- Evangelism is dependence, not performance.
- We trust the Spirit to do what only He can do.
- The goal of evangelism is the glory of Christ.
- We speak so that others may see Him as Savior and Lord.

Questions for Reflection and Practice

1. Where have you sensed the Spirit working in your life recently?
2. What is one small step of obedience you can take in sharing Christ this week?
3. Who can you pray with and walk alongside as you learn to witness to others?

Closing Thoughts

Jesus teaches us that no one comes to Him apart from the Spirit's drawing, and this truth shapes how we approach every conversation. Our role is to plant and water, but God alone gives the increase. This chapter reminds us to depend on the Spirit's power rather than our own persuasion or techniques. As you share the gospel, pray for the Spirit to open eyes, convict hearts, and reveal Christ clearly. Walk forward with confidence, knowing that the same Spirit who transformed your life is still at work in every heart you encounter.

Chapter 3

Scattering the Seed

Sowing the Word

Main Passage: Luke 8:4–15

Key Verse: *The seed is the word of God.* —Luke 8:11

The Sower and His Seed

A farmer walks into a field before sunrise. In his hand he carries seed—ordinary, unimpressive, small. He cannot control the weather. He cannot determine the soil. He cannot force growth. His task is simple: to scatter seed faithfully.

This is the picture Jesus gives us of evangelism. The seed represents the Word of God (v. 11). The soil represents the hearts of those who hear. Some hearts are hard, some shallow, some crowded, and some ready to receive. The condition of the heart is invisible to us but never hidden from God. Our role is not to examine the soil first or decide where growth seems most likely. Our role is to sow. We are not responsible for results; we are responsible for faithfulness.

The farmer does not sow because he is confident of the outcome; he sows because he trusts the power of the seed. In the same way, we do not share Christ because we feel persuasive or certain of how someone will respond. We share because the gospel is living and powerful, and because God uses His Word to awaken hearts, break up hard ground, and bring new life.

Evangelism is not about winning arguments or crafting perfect presentations. It is about placing the Word of God into the soil of the human heart and trusting the Spirit to work in ways we cannot see. The seed may take root slowly. It may sprout where we did not expect. It may grow long after we have walked away. But the power is in the seed, not in the sower. So we scatter. We trust. We wait. And we believe that God will give the increase.

Understanding the Soils

Not every seed takes root. Jesus made this clear. The issue was never the seed. The Word of God is always good. The difference was the condition of the soil.

Some hearts are hard. The Word lands, but it does not sink in. The past has wounded, pride has settled in, or sin has numbed the conscience. The gospel may be heard but is not received. This is not failure. It is simply soil that needs time and prayer.

Some hearts are shallow. There is initial excitement, interest, or emotion—but no depth. When difficulty appears, the growth withers. The root was never established. This is where patient discipleship matters.

Some hearts are crowded. The seed takes root, but the thorns of life—hurry, pain, pleasure, fear, distraction—choke out what God is doing. These are people who need not pressure but gentle guidance, space to breathe, and truth spoken with compassion.

And some hearts are ready, not because of us or because we explained things perfectly but because God has been preparing the soil long before we spoke. When the Word lands in such a heart, it takes root, grows, and bears fruit.

This understanding protects our hearts from both discouragement and pride. We do not judge our faithfulness by how quickly someone responds. We do not take credit when fruit appears, and we do not despair when it does not. We sow because the Word is powerful. We love because Christ loved us. We trust because the Spirit is working in unseen ways. Our role is not to control the soil. Our role is simply to sow faithfully.

The Patience of Sowing

Jesus said the good soil represents "those who, having heard the word with a noble and good heart, keep *it* and bear fruit with patience" (v. 15). Good soil is not something we find: it is something God forms. No one begins with a soft heart. Grace breaks ground. Conviction loosens the layers. The Spirit makes room for the seed to take root.

And once the seed is planted, growth is not instant. Seeds germinate beneath the surface where no one can see. The Spirit works in places we cannot observe and in ways we cannot measure. Our role is to trust that God is working, even when nothing seems to be happening. Jesus described this unseen work in the growth of a seed.

> *The kingdom of God is as if a man should scatter seed on the ground, and should sleep by night and rise by day, and the seed should sprout and grow, he himself does not know how. For the earth yields crops by itself: first the blade, then the head, after that the full grain in the head. But when the grain ripens, immediately he puts in the sickle, because the harvest has come.*
>
> —Mark 4:26–29

This frees us from rushing spiritual growth in others. We cannot hurry conviction. We cannot force repentance. We cannot demand fruit. We are not the gardener. We are the sower. The pace of growth belongs to God.

The field may look barren for a season. The soil may seem unchanged. The seed may appear forgotten. But the Word of God does not lie dormant without purpose. As Isaiah declares, it will accomplish what God intends (Isa. 55:11). So we keep sowing. We keep praying. We keep loving. We keep trusting. The seed is alive. The Spirit is working. The harvest is certain, even if unseen.

The Promise of Harvest

God sees every seed planted in faith. Even when we cannot measure progress, trace movement, or observe change, the Spirit is working in ways we cannot see. The growth of the kingdom is God's work, carried out in His timing and according to His wisdom.

This means that no conversation about Christ is wasted. No scripture shared is without purpose. No act of love is unnoticed. God uses each seed—some to soften the soil, some to awaken curiosity, some to expose need, and some to bring life. The gospel does its work even when the field appears unchanged.

There will be seasons where we sow with tears and seasons where we reap with joy (Ps. 126:5). Some harvests come quickly; others take years. Some seeds may not bear fruit until long after we are gone. But every seed of the Word carries the power of life, and God Himself is faithful to bring the harvest.

So we do not lose heart. We do not measure success by visible results. We do not carry the weight that belongs to God alone. We sow faithfully. We trust patiently. We rest confidently. For the God who called us to sow is the God who brings the increase.

Key Verses to Remember

Luke 8:11 – *The seed is the word of God.*

- The power in evangelism is in the Word, not the sower.

Hebrews 4:12 – *For the word of God* is *living and powerful, and sharper than any two-edged sword, piercing even to the division of soul and spirit . . . and is a discerner of the thoughts and intents of the heart.*

- The Word does what we cannot: It searches, pierces, and awakens.

Isaiah 55:11 – *So shall My word be that goes forth from My mouth; it shall not return to Me void, but it shall accomplish what I please.*

- God guarantees that His Word will do its work.

1 Corinthians 3:6 – *I planted, Apollos watered, but God gave the increase.*

- We labor faithfully, but God causes growth.

Galatians 6:9 – *And let us not grow weary while doing good, for in due season we shall reap if we do not lose heart.*

- The harvest may come slowly, but it will come.

Psalm 126:5–6 – *Those who sow in tears shall reap in joy. He who continually goes forth weeping . . . shall doubtless come again with rejoicing.*

- God sees every tear sown in love and will return it with joy.

Principles for Today

- The Word of God is the seed of new life.
- We are not sharing opinions or advice; we are planting truth.
- The condition of the heart determines the response.
- Our role is not to judge the soil but to faithfully sow into every life we encounter.
- Spiritual growth is often slow and unseen.
- God works beneath the surface long before we see visible change.
- Faithfulness matters more than visible results.
- We can sow and water, but only God can cause the seed to grow.
- Waiting is part of the work.
- Patience is not inactivity; it is trusting God's timing in the life of another.

- The harvest belongs to God.
- We sow in love, pray in hope, and rest in the confidence that God will bring the increase.

Questions for Reflection and Practice

1. Where do you see God inviting you to sow the Word in your daily life?
2. Are there people in your life who may need patience, prayer, and gentle conversation rather than pressure?
3. Who can you walk alongside in the work of sowing—someone to pray with, encourage, and labor with?

Closing Thoughts

Jesus reminds us that the power is in the seed, not the sower, and that faithfulness requires scattering the Word generously. We cannot control the soil, but we can ensure the gospel is shared with clarity and compassion. This chapter encourages you to persevere even when responses seem slow or discouraging. As you scatter the seed, trust that God is working in ways unseen and at a pace you may not understand. May you continue to sow with hope, confident that the Word of God never returns void.

PART 2

ENCOUNTERS WITH CHRIST

Learning from the Master's Conversations

Chapter 4

The New Birth

Reaching the Religious and Moral

Main Passage: John 3:1–21

Key Verse: *Unless one is born again, he cannot see the kingdom of God.* —John 3:3

A Nighttime Conversation

Nicodemus was a Pharisee, a ruler of the Jews, a man who had spent his life studying Scripture and striving to keep the law. As a respected teacher in Israel, he fasted, prayed, and gave faithfully. Outwardly, he was the model of morality and devotion. Yet beneath the robe of religion remained a restlessness he could not quiet. He had position but not peace, knowledge but not life.

Unlike others among the Pharisees who came to trap Jesus, Nicodemus approached Him sincerely. "Rabbi, we know that You are a teacher come from God; for no one can do these signs that You do unless God is with him" (v. 2). He recognized something divine in Jesus, but he still lacked what only Jesus could give.

The Necessity of the New Birth

Nicodemus was prepared for a theological discussion, but Jesus gave him a truth that cut through every religious assumption: "Unless one is born again, he cannot see the kingdom of God" (v. 3). Nicodemus understood repentance and ritual, but new birth was beyond anything he knew. He asked, "How can a man be born when he is old?" (v. 4). Jesus explained that this birth is a work of the Spirit, not human effort: "That which is born of the flesh is flesh, and that which is born of the Spirit is spirit" (v. 6).

Physical birth brings us into the world; spiritual birth brings us into God's family. The new birth is not turning over a new leaf; it is receiving a new life. It is not reform but regeneration (Titus 3:5). We often speak as if mankind simply needs a second chance, but Jesus says we need a second birth. This is not only necessary for the immoral, but for the moral, the religious, and the devout. "You must be born again" (v. 7).

The Mystery of the Spirit's Work

To illustrate the mystery of the new birth, Jesus pointed to the wind: "The wind blows where it wishes, and you hear the sound of it, but cannot tell where it comes from and where it goes" (v. 8). We cannot see the wind, yet we see its effects. We cannot predict its movement, yet we feel its power. So it is with the Spirit. The new birth is not the result of persuasion, emotion, or religious activity. It is God awakening the heart to believe. As John wrote in his prologue, "Who were born, not of blood, nor of the will of the flesh, nor of the will of man, but of God" (John 1:13). Our role is to witness; His role is to give life. Every genuine conversion is a quiet miracle—heaven breathing into a human soul.

The Failure of Religion to Save

Nicodemus was still confused. He asked, "How can these things be?" (v. 9). Jesus replied, "Are you the teacher of Israel, and do not know these things?" (v. 10). As a scholar of Scripture, Nicodemus should have recognized the promise God made through Ezekiel: "Then I will sprinkle clean water on you, and you shall be clean. . . . I will give you a new heart and put a new spirit within you. . . . I will put My Spirit within you and cause you to walk in My statutes" (Ezek. 36:25–27).

This was the very transformation Jesus was describing—cleansing from sin and the creation of a new heart, the gift of God's own Spirit indwelling believers and empowering them to walk out His commandments. Religion can polish the outside, but only God can make the heart new.

Nicodemus had discipline, morality, and religious status, but none of those produced life.

Jesus was not introducing a new doctrine but fulfilling an old one. The teacher of Israel had memorized the words but missed their meaning. Knowledge about God is not the same as life from God. Many today rest their hope in a gospel that has never changed them. They know the words of the gospel yet have never experienced its power. They mistake familiarity with faith. But Scripture says, "The Spirit Himself bears witness with our spirit that we are children of God" (Rom. 8:16). Assurance is not something we give ourselves or something an evangelist can give us. It is something the Spirit gives. Evangelism, therefore, must always point beyond religion to transformation—the new heart only God can give.

The Remedy from Heaven

After exposing Nicodemus's need, Jesus revealed the remedy: "As Moses lifted up the serpent in the wilderness, even so must the Son of Man be lifted up" (v. 14). He reached back to Numbers 21 and to a simple story that foreshadowed the gospel. Israel sinned, and deadly serpents filled the camp. The poison represented sin, and death was certain. God instructed Moses to lift a bronze serpent on a pole. Whoever looked at it lived—no ritual, no effort, just faith.

So it is with salvation. Humanity has been poisoned by sin, and only Christ lifted on the cross can save. The Spirit turns the sinner's eyes to Him, and the moment one believes, new life begins.

The Love That Gave All

Then Jesus spoke the words that have echoed ever since: "For God so loved the world that He gave His only begotten Son, that whoever believes in Him should not perish but have everlasting life" (v. 16). The gospel is not rooted in human effort but divine love. Christ did not come to condemn. The world was condemned already (v. 17). He came to rescue. The cross reveals the seriousness of sin and the magnitude of God's mercy.

The Division That Light Brings

Jesus closed with a solemn truth: "The light has come into the world, and men loved darkness rather than light" (v. 19). The gospel saves, but it also exposes. Some come to the light; others shrink back into darkness. Our task is not to force belief but to shine the light faithfully.

Recognizing the Religious and Moral

Nicodemus represents those who are religious, moral, and sincere, yet spiritually unchanged. They may respect Scripture, value church involvement, and speak the language of faith, but they lack the new birth Jesus described. Their confidence in their goodness or religious history keeps them from recognizing their need for a transformed heart. These individuals are often closer than others to embracing truth, but they must first see that salvation is not earned—it is given.

How to Recognize Them

These individuals can often be recognized by the way they:

- Ask thoughtful spiritual questions yet remain unsure of what they truly need.
- Rely on morality, good works, or religious tradition as evidence that they are right with God.
- Approach spiritual conversations intellectually rather than personally.
- Show deep respect for Jesus while resisting the idea of personal repentance.
- Feel confused or even defensive when confronted with truths that challenge their assumptions.
- Believe they are spiritually secure because of their religious identity or upbringing.

How to Engage Them

When speaking with them, it is helpful to:

- Affirm their desire for truth while gently exposing the limits of religion and morality.

- Redirect the conversation from outward obedience to inward transformation.
- Explain the new birth using simple biblical language (Ezek. 36:26–27; John 3:5–8)
- Ask questions that reveal whether their confidence is in Christ or in themselves.
- Avoid arguments and keep pointing to the necessity of spiritual rebirth.
- Emphasize that salvation is received through faith, not achieved through effort.
- Share testimonies of people who discovered that religion cannot replace regeneration.

What They Might Say

- "I try to live right and follow God's commandments."
- "I've always believed in God and gone to church."
- "I pray every day."
- "I've always been a religious person."

Those who are religious and moral need to see that goodness cannot make them right with God. They must be gently shown that salvation comes not through effort or tradition but through the new birth that only Christ can give.

Bringing It Home: Using This in Practice

When you meet a "Nicodemus," your goal is not to win a debate but to reveal the difference between religion and regeneration. Jesus didn't shame Nicodemus – He guided him to truth. We must do the same. Focus on the heart, not the performance.

If someone says, "I've always believed in God," you could respond, "That's a great start, but Jesus told Nicodemus that knowledge alone isn't enough. What do you think He meant when He said, 'You must be born again'?"

This gently invites reflection on their experience, not their information.

If they say, "I go to church and pray every day," you might say, "That's good, but Nicodemus did too. He was a respected teacher of the law, yet Jesus said he still needed something new inside. Have you ever thought about what that means for us?"

This shifts the focus from religion to regeneration.

If they say, "I've always been a Christian," you can respond, "I used to feel that way too, but Jesus said the new birth is something God does in us—not something we're born into. Would you like to know what He meant by that?"

This opens the door to explain the work of the Holy Spirit and new life in Christ.

When you speak to religious people, emphasize what Jesus emphasized—that entrance into God's kingdom requires a heart transformed by the Spirit, not just a mind filled with truth.

Key Verses to Remember

John 3:3 – *Unless one is born again, he cannot see the kingdom of God.*

- The new birth is not optional; no amount of moral effort, religious activity, or sincerity can replace it.

John 3:6 – *That which is born of the flesh is flesh, and that which is born of the Spirit is spirit.*

- Spiritual life cannot be produced by human effort; it is the work of the Spirit alone.

John 1:13 – *Who were born, not of blood, nor of the will of the flesh, nor of the will of man, but of God.*

- Spiritual birth does not come from heritage, personal discipline, or human decision; it is a work of God.

Ezekiel 36:26 – *I will give you a new heart and put a new spirit within you.*

- The new birth was always God's plan, promised long before Christ came; true change begins from the inside out.

2 Corinthians 5:17 – *If anyone* is *in Christ,* he is *a new creation.*

- When God gives new life, the result is transformation—not just improved behavior but changed identity.

Romans 8:16 – *The Spirit Himself bears witness with our spirit that we are children of God.*

- True salvation comes with inward assurance from the Holy Spirit, not the fragile confidence of outward religion.

Principles for Today

- The new birth is essential for everyone.
- Only God can give spiritual life.
- The work of the Spirit is unseen but undeniable.
- True conversion results in a transformed heart.
- Biblical knowledge must lead to spiritual encounter.
- Knowing about God is not the same as knowing Him.
- Assurance of salvation is the Spirit's work, not ours.
- The Spirit confirms new life within the believer.
- The cross is the only cure for the poison of sin.
- Sinners must look to Christ alone for salvation.
- God's love invites every heart to come.
- Salvation is offered freely to all who believe.
- The gospel brings both light and decision.
- Christ exposes darkness to call sinners to life.

Closing Thoughts

Jesus reveals that true salvation is a supernatural work of God, not the result of human effort or religious performance. Recognizing this frees us from pressure and focuses our conversations on the heart's need for spiritual transformation. This chapter calls us to present the gospel clearly, inviting others to experience the new birth only God can give. As you engage the religious and moral, trust the Spirit to break through their confidence and reveal their need for grace. May you speak boldly and humbly, knowing that God alone brings the spiritually dead to life.

Chapter 5

LIVING WATER

Reaching the Broken and Thirsty

Main Passage: John 4:1–30

Key Verse: *Whoever drinks of the water that I shall give him will never thirst.* —John 4:14

A Divine Appointment

Jesus' journey through Samaria was no coincidence. John tells us that He needed to go through that region (v. 4). The need was not geographical; it was relational. Grace had an appointment at a well. The woman came alone at the hottest part of the day, carrying her water jar and her shame. Jesus was already there, waiting. The One who spoke the worlds into existence positioned Himself at a well to reach one wounded heart. Evangelism often begins with God placing us in the right place, at the right moment, to speak to one person.

Going Where Others Avoid

Most Jews avoided Samaria, traveling miles out of their way to stay clear of the people they despised. But Jesus went where others refused to go. He stepped into the places that religion avoided because that was where the broken were. Jesus said, "Those who are well have no need of a physician, but those who are sick. I did not come to call *the* righteous, but sinners, to repentance" (Mark 2:17). If we want to reach the people Jesus reached, we must go where Jesus went. The thirsty are rarely found in the places that feel comfortable. Evangelism requires movement toward the wounded, not retreat from them.

Crossing Barriers to Reach the Heart

When Jesus said, "Give Me a drink," He crossed every barrier of His culture—ethnic, religious, gender, and moral. The Samaritan woman expected avoidance; instead, she received attention. Evangelism begins with compassion, not correction. It begins not with proving truth but by opening a door for truth to be heard. Sometimes the most powerful first step is simply showing attention, asking a question, or listening without judgment. Love speaks first.

From Physical Water to Living Water

The woman misunderstood Jesus' offer of "living water." She was thinking of wells, buckets, and daily labor, but Jesus was speaking of a much deeper thirst. Every person carries a thirst of the soul—a longing for peace, identity, love, forgiveness, and purpose. We try to satisfy that thirst in many ways: relationships, success, approval, pleasure, and distraction. But none of these can reach the places where the heart aches the most.

Jesus said, "If you knew the gift of God, and who it is . . . you would have asked" (v. 10). The issue was not desire; it was awareness. If she knew who He was, she would have asked Him for the very thing her soul had been longing for.

This is the heart of evangelism. We are not trying to force belief or persuade people into religion. We are helping them recognize the true source of what they are already searching for. As Jesus continued speaking, her curiosity became desire. "Sir, give me this water" (v. 15). Her thirst was awakened.

Exposing the Wound

Once her thirst awakened, Jesus touched the place where her heart was truly aching. He said to her, "Go, call your husband" (v. 16). She replied, "I have no husband." And Jesus answered, "You have well said, 'I have no husband,' for you have had five husbands, and the one whom you now have is not your husband" (vv. 17–18). Jesus was not humiliating her. He was revealing the well she had been drinking from. She had tried to satisfy her thirst through relationships. Each one promised fulfillment; each one left her empty.

Jesus did not expose her wound to shame her, but to heal her. Truth without love crushes, and love without truth cannot save. Jesus brought both. Before the gospel can heal, it must uncover what is being hidden.

Redirecting Religious Diversions

Conviction is uncomfortable, and the woman tried to change the subject. "Our fathers worshiped on this mountain, and you *Jews* say that in Jerusalem is the place where one ought to worship" (v. 20). It was a diversion, an attempt to replace conviction with conversation.

When the heart begins to stir, people often pivot to religion, politics, denominational differences, or some other diversion.

"What church do you go to?"
"What denomination are you?"
"There are too many hypocrites."

These are modern versions of the same deflection. Jesus did not debate her. He redirected her to the heart of the matter: "True worshipers will worship the Father in spirit and truth" (v. 23). He moved the focus from where to how, from external forms to internal faith. True worship is not confined by mountains, temples, or denominations. It is the outflow of a heart made alive by truth. We must not allow ourselves to chase theological rabbits down endless trails. Keep steering the conversation back to the person of Christ and the posture of the heart.

The Revelation of the Savior

True worship happens when the real you comes before the real God—not the polished, guarded, church version of you but the you who is broken, thirsty, tired, wounded, ashamed, or searching. The you who knows things aren't okay. The you who is honest.

And the God who meets us there is not the god we invent—the one who never confronts and never transforms. True worship happens when we come as we are before the God who is—the God who is holy, loving, present, and true. God is not impressed with performance, and He is not fooled by pretending. Worship begins where honesty meets holiness.

It was in that place when her defenses fell and her heart opened that Jesus revealed Himself. When the woman mentioned the coming Messiah, Jesus said plainly, "I who speak to you am *He*" (v. 26).

And this is the aim of every gospel conversation—not to win an argument, not to prove a point, not to deliver information, but to introduce a person to the Savior. Our goal is not to get them to adopt a system, change behavior, or agree with our reasoning. Our goal is to help the thirsty see the One who gives living water.

The Overflow of a Changed Life

The woman left her waterpot behind. She walked away from the very thing she used to draw from a well that never satisfied. The waterpot represented her old way of trying to quench her thirst. When she encountered the One who could truly satisfy her, she no longer needed what she once depended on. Salvation not only fills; it replaces. It changes where we go for comfort, identity, and worth.

And the change didn't stay private. The same woman who avoided the crowd now ran toward the very people she had been hiding from. She cried out, "Come see a Man" (v. 29). When shame is replaced by grace, silence is replaced by testimony. When Christ satisfies the soul, the gospel overflows. Evangelism isn't something we perform; it's the natural response of a heart that has finally found water.

Recognizing the Broken and Thirsty

The Samaritan woman represents those who carry deep wounds, hidden guilt, and long histories of brokenness. They often conceal their pain behind humor, avoidance, or a hardened exterior, yet beneath the surface lies a longing for healing and acceptance. Their shame isolates them, and they may believe their failures disqualify them from God's love. Jesus shows that these individuals do not need condemnation; they need hope, grace, and the assurance that living water is offered even to the most broken.

How to Recognize Them

These individuals can often be recognized by the way they:

- Avoid spiritual conversations by shifting topics or deflecting with humor.
- Carry emotional scars connected to relationships, guilt, or trauma.
- Hide behind sarcasm or tough attitudes to protect themselves from vulnerability.
- Feel unworthy of God due to their past or their current struggles.
- Avoid religious environments out of fear of judgment or exposure.

How to Engage Them

When speaking with them, it is helpful to:

- Lead with compassion, showing them they are seen and valued.
- Avoid harsh language and judgment; their hearts are already bruised.
- Ask gentle questions that uncover thirst rather than expose sin harshly.
- Emphasize God's grace, acceptance, and desire to restore the broken.

- Share scriptures that highlight Christ's compassion toward the hurting.
- Affirm that Jesus knows their story fully and still invites them to come.
- Focus on the hope of forgiveness, healing, and transformation available in Christ.

What They Might Say

- "If you knew what I've done, you'd understand why God wouldn't want me."
- "I've messed up too many times."
- "I just try not to think of my past."
- "Why would God care about someone like me?"
- "I don't deserve anything from God."

Those who are wounded and ashamed need to know that Jesus sees them fully and offers grace, not rejection. They must experience a Savior who meets them in their brokenness and gives living water that heals the deepest parts of their soul.

Bringing It Home: Using This in Practice

When you meet a "Samaritan woman," your goal isn't to condemn their thirst but to help them recognize who they are truly thirsty for. Jesus didn't start by preaching about sin;

He started by asking for water. His request opened the door for a conversation about her deeper need. We can follow His example by beginning where people are and lovingly leading them toward the water that truly satisfies.

If someone says, "I just want to be happy."

You could respond, "We all long for that. Jesus once spoke with someone who felt that same emptiness. Can I share how He met her need?"

This shifts the focus from temporary happiness to lasting fulfillment.

If they say, "Relationships always disappoint me."

You might say, "That's a pain many people carry. Jesus talked with a woman who had been wounded in the same way. Would you like to hear what He offered her?"

This connects their wound to Christ's compassion, not His correction.

If they say, "I've made too many mistakes for God to care about me."

You can respond, "The woman Jesus met at the well felt exactly that, but Jesus didn't avoid her; He came to her. Would you like to hear what He said to her?"

This moves the conversation from shame to invitation.

If they say, "I've tried religion; it didn't work."

You could say, "Jesus didn't offer her religion. He offered her living water, a relationship that satisfies the heart. Can I show you what He meant by that?"

We do not hand thirsty souls a lecture. We help them recognize their thirst—and point them to the well.

Key Verses to Remember

John 4:14 – *But whoever drinks of the water that I shall give him will never thirst.*

- Only Jesus can satisfy the deepest thirst of the soul.

Psalm 63:1 – *My soul thirsts for You . . . in a dry and thirsty land.*

- The heart was created to thirst for God.

Jeremiah 2:13 – *They have forsaken Me, the fountain of living waters,* and *hewn themselves cisterns—broken cisterns that can hold no water.*

- Everything we turn to besides God ultimately fails to satisfy.

Matthew 5:6 – *Blessed* are *those who hunger and thirst for righteousness, for they shall be filled.*

- God promises to satisfy those who seek Him.

John 6:35 – *He who believes in Me shall never thirst.*

- Jesus is the source of lasting fulfillment.

Revelation 22:17 – *And let him who thirsts come.*

- The invitation to drink is open to all who are thirsty.

Principles for Today

- No one is beyond the reach of grace.
- Jesus seeks the wounded and the weary.
- Evangelism begins with compassion, not condemnation.
- Love opens doors that arguments cannot.
- Ordinary moments can become divine appointments.
- God places us where thirsty souls can be found.
- Jesus leads from physical need to spiritual truth.
- Begin where people are, then lift their eyes higher.
- True worship flows from a transformed heart.
- God desires sincerity, not just religious practice.
- A changed life naturally becomes a witness.
- When Jesus satisfies the soul, the gospel overflows.

Closing Thoughts

Jesus shows His compassion for the wounded and ashamed, meeting them at the point of their deepest thirst. His approach reminds us that hurting people need both truth and tenderness as they wrestle with their past. This chapter invites you to offer living water to those who feel unworthy or forgotten.

As you engage with compassion, trust that Christ can heal what shame has wounded and restore what sin has broken. May you walk forward with gentleness, pointing every thirsty soul to the One who satisfies forever.

Chapter 6

The Mirror of the Law

Reaching the Self-Righteous and Blind

Main Passage: Mark 10:17–22

Key Verse: *No one* is *good but One,* that is, *God.* —Mark 10:18

A Sincere Seeker

If most believers could script the perfect gospel encounter, it would look like this one. A man runs to Jesus, kneels before Him, and asks how to inherit eternal life. He is eager, respectful, sincere, and spiritually curious. He asks the right question, and he seems ready to submit.

Many evangelists today would have gone straight to the gospel or a sinner's prayer, but Jesus didn't do that. Instead of offering grace first, He offered the law. He did not comfort the man's sincerity; He confronted his self-righteousness. This surprises us because we forget something crucial: The gospel is not received by the righteous but by those who know they are sinners (Mark 2:17). Grace means nothing until guilt becomes personal. Before Jesus could save him, He had to redefine goodness.

Misunderstanding Goodness

The conversation begins with one revealing phrase: "Good Teacher" (v. 17). The ruler believed that goodness was something measured and achieved, something both he and Jesus possessed. But Jesus stopped him, saying, "Why do you call Me good? No one *is* good but One, *that is*, God" (v. 18). Jesus was not denying His deity; He was exposing the man's definition of goodness.

The ruler believed goodness was something you arrive at, something you become by doing the right things and avoiding the wrong ones. We see this in his question: "What good thing shall I do?" (Matt. 19:16). His assumption was the same assumption that nearly all people carry: If I am not good enough yet, I can become good enough. This is the natural religion of the human heart. "There is a way *that seems* right to a man, but its end *is* the way of death" (Prov. 14:12). Many believe they can adjust, improve, tweak, or mature into moral sufficiency. In their view, goodness is something earned.

People also define goodness by comparing themselves to others, just like the Pharisee who prayed, "God, I thank You that I am not like other men" (Luke 18:11). Comparison is the cornerstone of self-righteousness. But God's standard is not being better than others; it is being perfect like Him (Matt. 5:48). Our goodness ends the moment the comparison shifts from other people to God Himself. Standing in front of Jesus, the embodiment of perfect righteousness, the ruler's goodness was exposed as insufficient.

Holding Up the Mirror of the Law

Jesus pointed the man to the commandments, not as a path to salvation but as a mirror of truth: "You know the commandments" (v. 19). The ruler confidently replied, "All these things I have kept from my youth" (v. 20). He saw the law as a ladder to climb toward heaven. Jesus used it as a mirror to show how far he had fallen. Romans 3:20 declares, "By the deeds of the law no flesh will be justified . . . for by the law *is* the knowledge of sin." The law cannot cleanse; it can only reveal. Like a mirror showing a dirty face, it exposes the stain but provides no soap.

In conversation, we can do what Jesus did: lovingly hold up the mirror of the law. When someone says, "I'm a good person," you can ask:

- "Have you ever told a lie?"
- "Have you ever stolen anything?"
- "Have you ever used God's name as a curse word?"

- "Have you ever dishonored your parents?"
- "Have you ever lusted?" (Matt. 5:27–28)
- "Have you ever hated someone?" (Matt. 5:21–22)

By asking these questions, we are not condemning them; we are letting the Word of God and the Holy Spirit bring conviction. James wrote, "For whoever shall keep the whole law, and yet stumble in *one* point, he is guilty of all" (James. 2:10–11). Breaking one commandment is rebellion against the Lawgiver Himself. That is why Jesus said, "Therefore you shall be perfect, just as your Father in heaven is perfect" (Matt. 5:48). If someone wants to reach heaven by their own goodness, perfection—not sincerity—is the requirement.

The Crowbar of Conviction

When the ruler asked, "What do I still lack?" (Matt. 19:20), the law had already begun to pry at his conscience. That question revealed the crack forming in his self-confidence. He was beginning to sense that his goodness was not as solid as he once believed.

This is the purpose of the law. It is not given to make us righteous, but to reveal that we are not. The law exalts God's holiness while humbling man, showing us the infinite distance between who God is and who we are. It lifts God up and brings us down, exposing the rebellion we cannot see on our own. Scripture says, "The law of the Lord *is* perfect, converting the soul" (Ps. 19:7). The perfection of the law reveals the imperfection of the heart. The law removes every excuse by bringing awareness to sin and exposing our guilt before God (Rom. 3:19–20).

Evangelism that skips conviction builds false conversions; evangelism that applies the law in love prepares the heart for genuine faith. Our task is not to crush people with guilt but to uncover the truth that drives them to grace.

When the Gospel Must Wait

Mark writes, "Jesus, looking at him, loved him" (v. 21). That line changes everything. Jesus loved the man deeply, yet He didn't lead him in a sinner's prayer. Instead, He pressed right where the god of his heart was hidden: "Sell whatever you have and give to the poor . . . and come . . . follow Me" (v. 21). Rather than give him the gospel, Jesus gave him another command, revealing the futility of trying to earn righteousness through works. The man went away sorrowful, not because he didn't understand but because he understood perfectly. Grace was ready, but he was not.

Sometimes the most Christlike thing we can do is stop and let the law speak. Until a person sees the sinfulness of sin, he will never see the beauty of the Savior. You won't go to Lowe's to buy a new faucet until you realize the old one is leaking. The law shows us that we are leaking so we will look beyond ourselves for a Savior. And though the law cannot save us, it will take us by the hand and lead us to the One who can. Paul wrote, "Therefore the law was our tutor *to bring us* to Christ, that we might be justified by faith" (Gal. 3:24). Only when guilt becomes personal does grace become a treasure.

Recognizing the Self-Righteous and Blind

The rich young ruler represents those who are confident in their goodness yet blind to their true spiritual condition. They measure themselves by their morality, achievements, or religious performance, and believe they have met God's standard. Their sincerity is real, but their self-righteousness keeps them from seeing their need for grace. These individuals must be gently confronted with the law so they can recognize their sin and understand that eternal life cannot be earned.

How to Recognize Them

These individuals can often be recognized by the way they:

- Speak confidently about keeping God's commandments or living a moral life.
- Compare themselves to others and conclude they are "better than most."
- Minimize sin by focusing on outward behavior rather than the heart.
- Resist the idea that they fall short spiritually.
- Become defensive when confronted with God's holiness or their need for repentance.

- Believe eternal life is something to be achieved rather than received.

How to Engage Them

When speaking with them, it is helpful to:

- Use the law gently to reveal the true condition of the heart.
- Help them see sin not just as outward actions but as inward attitudes and desires.
- Emphasize that no one can meet God's perfect standard apart from Christ.
- Avoid debating morality and instead point them to God's holiness.
- Ask questions that expose underlying pride and self-reliance.
- Show them how Jesus fulfilled the law on their behalf (Rom. 8:3–4).
- Highlight the difference between obedience that earns and obedience that flows from salvation.

What They Might Say

- "I've always tried to live a good life."
- "I follow the Ten Commandments the best I can."
- "I try to follow the Golden Rule."

- "I don't sin as much as some people."
- "I know I'm a good person."
- "I'm doing everything I can to get to heaven."
- "What else do I need to do?"

Those who are self-righteous and blind must see that the law is a mirror—revealing sin, not removing it. They need to realize that eternal life is not achieved through goodness but received through Christ alone.

Bringing It Home: Using This in Practice

When you meet a "rich young ruler," your goal isn't to argue, shame, or expose their sin publicly but to gently dismantle their illusion of goodness. Don't rush to share the good news right away. Instead, hold up the mirror of God's law—not to defeat them but to awaken need. They don't need convincing that Jesus was good; they need revealing that they are not. The law is not our enemy; it is the doorway to grace. When the law is shared with love, the Spirit uses it to break pride and prepare the heart for mercy.

If someone says, "I think I'll go to heaven because I try to be a good person."

You could respond, "Trying to be good is admirable. But Jesus said, 'No one is good but One, that is, God.' Can I share with you what that means?"

This shifts the standard from our goodness to God's goodness, revealing the need for grace.

If they say, "I've always tried to do what is right."

You might say, "That's a sincere desire. The rich young ruler said something similar, but Jesus showed him that doing what is right on the outside isn't the same as having a heart that's truly right before God. Can I show you how Jesus revealed the difference?"

This invites them to see that righteousness is not achieved by effort but received through Christ.

If they say, "I know I have my faults, but I'm not as bad as some people."

You can respond, "We can always find someone worse to compare ourselves to, but Jesus said that the standard is God Himself, not other people. He told us to 'be perfect as your Father in heaven is perfect.' How do you think you compare to Him?"

This redirects the comparison from other people to God Himself.

If they say, "God knows my heart."

You could say, "He does, and that's exactly why we need mercy. Can I ask you a few questions?" (Then hold up the mirror of the law. "Have you ever told a lie?" and so on).

This helps them see sin not as accusation but as honest self-reflection, opening the heart for grace.

We don't use the law as a club to strike people down. We use it as a crowbar to open the heart so grace can enter.

Key Verses to Remember

Mark 10:18 – *No one* is *good but One,* that is, *God.*

- Goodness is measured by God's holiness.

Proverbs 14:12 – *There is a way* that seems *right to a man, but its end* is *the way of death.*

- Our natural sense of goodness leads us away from God, not toward Him.

James 2:10 – *For whoever shall keep the whole law, and yet stumble in one point, he is guilty of all.*

- One sin reveals our guilt and need for mercy.

Matthew 5:48 – *Therefore you shall be perfect, just as your Father in heaven is perfect.*

- God's standard is not sincerity or effort; it is perfection.

Romans 3:20 – *For by the law* is *the knowledge of sin.*

- The law shows us our sin; it cannot save us from it.

Galatians 3:24 – *Therefore the law was our tutor* to bring us *to Christ, that we might be justified by faith.*

- The purpose of the law is to lead us to Christ, not to self-righteousness.

Principles for Today

- Most people are not rejecting Jesus; they simply think they don't need Him.
- Self-righteousness blinds the heart to its true condition.
- The law is not the enemy of grace; it prepares the heart for grace.
- It exposes our sin so Christ becomes our only hope.
- Do not rush to offer forgiveness before guilt is understood.
- The gospel only becomes good news when we realize we need it.
- The Spirit uses the Word to awaken conviction.
- Our role is to speak truth gently and trust Him to work in the heart.
- Our goal is not to win arguments but to awaken need.
- We exalt God's holiness so Christ may be treasured.

Closing Thoughts

Jesus uses the law to expose the hidden pride of the self-righteous, revealing their need for a Savior rather than self-reform. His example teaches us to speak truth with love, helping others see the gap between outward morality and inward holiness. This chapter encourages you to hold up the mirror of God's law with wisdom and patience. As you engage those who trust in their own goodness, pray for clarity and conviction that leads them to grace. May you faithfully guide them toward the only righteousness that saves—Christ's, not their own.

Chapter 7

RELIGION WITHOUT MERCY

Reaching the Self-Justifying

Main Passage: Luke 10:25–37

Key Verse: *But he, wanting to justify himself, said to Jesus, "And who is my neighbor?"*—Luke 10:29

A Legal Expert Meets the Lord

A lawyer once stood before Jesus with a question that sounded humble but was loaded with pride: "Teacher, what shall I do to inherit eternal life?" (v. 25). It was the same question asked by the rich young ruler but for a different reason. The ruler was searching for one more deed to add to his list of virtues; the lawyer was searching for a loophole. Both wanted to justify themselves, but they arrived at that desire from opposite directions. One thought he had done enough; the other hoped the requirements weren't too much.

Jesus answered both men in the same way: by pointing them to the law. Yet His intent was not to confirm their goodness but to confront their hearts. The ruler needed to see that his obedience was incomplete, while the lawyer needed to see that his definition of love was too small. Jesus asked, "What is written in the law? What is your reading *of it*?" (v. 26). The lawyer quoted the right verse, the one that summarized the entire law: love God completely and love your neighbor as yourself. His knowledge was precise, but his heart was partial. He loved God in theory but not in practice. He loved the idea of neighborliness but not the people who made that idea inconvenient.

The Limits of Lawful Love

Having answered correctly, the lawyer should have stopped there. But Scripture says, "But he, wanting to justify himself, said to Jesus, 'And who is my neighbor?'" (v. 29). That question revealed everything. He wasn't seeking to love more; he was looking to love less. His goal was not to understand God's standard but to narrow it until he could meet it. In his mind, if he could define "neighbor" as only those like himself, then his righteousness would remain intact.

This is where the self-justifying heart always goes: toward limitation rather than liberation. It tries to shrink God's commands to fit within human comfort. Instead of asking, "How can I love like God loves?" it asks, "Who do I really have to love?" This pattern appears today when people say, "I treat everyone fairly" or "I help those who deserve it." That spirit measures compassion by merit instead of mercy. It keeps love within the borders of preference, culture, or convenience.

For those learning to share their faith, this moment in the story is instructive. Jesus didn't debate the lawyer's definitions or lecture on theology. He told a story that dismantled every excuse. Evangelism often requires the same wisdom: to speak truth in a way that bypasses argument and reaches the conscience. When someone wants to justify themselves, reasoning alone won't reach them; only the truth that exposes the heart will.

The Parable That Exposed the Heart

Jesus answered the lawyer's question, not with a definition but with a story. A man was traveling from Jerusalem to Jericho when he fell among thieves and was beaten and left for dead. Both a priest and a Levite saw him but passed by on the other side. Each man represented a form of religion that keeps its distance. They could quote the law of love but refused to be inconvenienced by it. Then came a Samaritan, the very kind of man the lawyer would have despised. He stopped, stooped, and served. He bandaged wounds, gave his own resources, and promised to return.

This story didn't just describe mercy; it redefined it. The question was, "Who is my neighbor?" but Jesus turned it around: "Which of these three do you think was neighbor to him who fell among the thieves?" (v. 36). The difference is subtle but piercing. The lawyer asked, "Who qualifies to be loved?" Jesus asked, "What kind of person are you willing to be?" True love is not determined by the worthiness of the recipient but by the character of the giver. The Samaritan crossed barriers of race, religion, and reputation, and in doing so, he reflected the very heart of Christ who came to those the world overlooked.

For the evangelist, this story teaches that love opens the door where argument cannot. Many people, like the lawyer, hide behind intellect or morality, but compassion breaks through self-defense. The story of the Good Samaritan shows that the gospel is not confined to those who look like us or think like us. It is love in action—love that crosses the street, stoops to serve, and pays the cost of mercy.

The Measure of Love

When Jesus finished the story, conviction replaced confidence. The lawyer couldn't bring himself to say the word "Samaritan." Instead, he replied, "He who showed mercy on him" (v. 37). It was an admission of truth that cut through his pride. The one he would have least expected to be righteous was the only one who truly acted in love. Jesus then said, "Go and do likewise" (v. 37). The words were simple, but they carried the full weight of the gospel's demand.

This was not a call to imitation but to transformation. Jesus wasn't telling the lawyer to try harder; He was showing him that such love was impossible without a changed heart. The kind of mercy displayed by the Samaritan is not born from moral effort; it flows from divine compassion. The law can reveal what love requires, but only grace can produce it.

In that moment, the lawyer stood face to face with the One who embodied the story. Jesus Himself is the true Samaritan—moved with compassion, crossing the distance between heaven and earth, binding the wounds of sin, and paying the full cost of redemption.

For those who share the gospel, this is the same measure of love. Evangelism is not simply about telling others what to believe; it is demonstrating the heart of Christ in how we approach them. People rarely remember our arguments, but they never forget our mercy. The same Spirit who filled Jesus with compassion now fills His people with power to love beyond human limits. The world measures love by feelings or familiarity; God measures love by sacrifice. When believers love those who oppose them, forgive those who wound them, and serve those who cannot repay, they reflect the Savior's love—and that love becomes the gospel's greatest witness.

Recognizing the Self-Justifying

The lawyer represents those who use religious knowledge to justify themselves rather than to seek truth. They are skilled at defining terms, debating theology, and shifting the focus away from their own hearts. Their questions often sound sincere, but their motive is to appear righteous rather than be made right with God. Jesus exposes this tendency by revealing that true love flows from a transformed heart, not from self-defense or intellectual maneuvering.

How to Recognize Them

These individuals can often be recognized by the way they:

- Use theological questions to deflect conviction rather than pursue truth.
- Shift conversations toward definitions, technicalities, or hypotheticals.
- Look for loopholes in God's commands to avoid personal responsibility.
- Compare themselves favorably to others to excuse their lack of obedience.
- Treat spiritual conversations like debates rather than matters of the heart.
- Emphasize what they already know instead of what God is revealing.

How to Engage Them

When speaking to them, it is helpful to:

- Bring the conversation back to the heart rather than abstract ideas.
- Ask questions that uncover motives, not just opinions.
- Use Scripture to expose the gap between knowledge and obedience.

- Avoid getting lost in debates or word games that distract from the gospel.
- Highlight Jesus' emphasis on compassion, humility, and genuine love.
- Invite them to consider whether their "righteousness" has produced Christ-like character.
- Show them that salvation is not found in justifying themselves but in trusting Christ.

What They Might Say

- "Well, it depends on what you mean by . . . "
- "I already know that verse. What else do you have?"
- "But technically, do I really have to . . . ?"
- "Other people don't do that, so why should I?"
- "I understand the Bible. I'm fine."
- "There has to be another way to interpret that."

Those who are self-justifying need to see that knowledge without obedience leads to spiritual blindness. They must be confronted with the truth that salvation comes not through defending themselves but through surrendering to the mercy of Christ.

Bringing It Home: Using This in Practice

When you meet a person like this, the goal is not to win an argument but to tell a story that reveals mercy or ask a question that makes truth personal. Jesus didn't correct the lawyer's theology. He invited him into a narrative that broke through his pride. Truth wrapped in compassion disarms self-defense and invites the heart to see itself honestly.

If someone says, "I try to treat people right. That's what really matters."

You might respond, "That's good. Jesus said the greatest commandment is to love God and love our neighbor. Can I share a story He told about what that love looks like?"

This gently shifts the focus from their definition of goodness to Jesus' description of mercy.

If someone says, "I think being kind and fair is enough."

You might say, "That's what the religious leaders thought too, but Jesus showed them that love goes further than fairness. Can I share with you a story He told?"

This opens the door for the Good Samaritan story and helps reveal that love is measured by sacrifice.

If someone says, "People should just take care of their own."

You could respond, "That's what most people believed in Jesus' day too, but He told a story that turned that idea upside down. Can I share it with you?"

This introduces the conversation naturally and challenges assumptions without confrontation.

Stories like the Good Samaritan help people see that God's love goes farther than human effort and that His mercy is what every heart truly needs.

Key Verses to Remember

Luke 10:27 – *You shall love the Lord your God with all your heart, with all your soul, with all your strength, and with all your mind,' and 'your neighbor as yourself.'*

- God's standard of love leaves no room for self-justification; it calls for total devotion and unconditional mercy.

James 2:13 – *For judgment is without mercy to the one who has shown no mercy. Mercy triumphs over judgment.*

- God's people reflect His heart when mercy outweighs criticism and compassion silences condemnation.

1 John 4:20–21 – *If someone says, "I love God," and hates his brother, he is a liar; for he who does not love his brother whom he has seen, how can he love God whom he has not seen?*

- True love for God is proven by how we treat others. Love for Him and love for people cannot be separated.

Romans 13:10 – *Love does no harm to a neighbor; therefore love* is *the fulfillment of the law.*

- The law's ultimate goal is not regulation but transformation—to shape hearts that act in mercy.

John 13:34–35 – *A new commandment I give to you, that you love one another; as I have loved you, that you also love one another. By this all will know that you are My disciples, if you have love for one another.*

- Our love for others becomes the evidence of Christ's presence within us.

Principles for Today

- Self-justification always shrinks the scope of love.
- It looks for boundaries instead of opportunities.
- True love crosses every barrier.
- Mercy moves toward need, not comfort.
- Knowing truth is not enough.
- Love must take shape in action.
- Compassion reaches where arguments cannot.
- Mercy disarms pride more than reasoning ever will.
- The gospel calls us to embody what we share.
- Our message of love is proven by how we love.

Closing Thoughts

Jesus confronts the self-justifying heart by bringing the conversation back to compassion, obedience, and genuine love. His example teaches us that knowledge without transformation is empty and powerless. This chapter invites you to engage those who defend themselves with arguments rather than humility. As you speak, trust God to reveal the deeper issues beneath their questions and objections. May you gently guide them toward a faith that moves beyond words and is proven by mercy, surrender, and obedience to Christ.

Chapter 8

Grace in the Dust

Reaching the Guilty and Condemned

Main Passage: John 8:1–11

Key Verse: *Neither do I condemn you; go and sin no more.* —John 8:11

Caught in the Crossfire

The woman caught in adultery was not seeking Jesus; she was dragged to Him. She was guilty. No excuses. No defense. No place to hide. But her accusers weren't interested in justice or repentance. In their hands she was a pawn, a tool to discredit Jesus. They threw her into the center of the crowd and forced her shame into public view. She felt fear and humiliation as every eye fixed upon her and every hand carried a stone. The law was clear. Death felt inevitable. The trap was set.

What would Jesus do? Would He uphold the law and contradict His message of grace, mercy, and forgiveness?

Or would He show mercy and violate the very law He wrote? It was here, in this moment, that the law and the gospel seemed to collide, yet Jesus would teach us how grace meets guilt without compromising truth.

This scene exposes more than the woman's guilt. It exposes the hearts of everyone present. The religious leaders used the law as a weapon, not a guide. The crowd watched with curiosity, not compassion. And the woman stood crushed beneath both condemnation and fear. Yet Jesus stepped into the tension with perfect wisdom. For the evangelist, this moment teaches us how to bring grace and truth to those who feel trapped by their sin, shamed by others, or crushed under the weight of their past.

The Weight of the Law

The scribes and the Pharisees believed they had placed Jesus in an impossible position. Moses commanded that such a woman be stoned, so if Jesus upheld the law, His reputation as a friend of sinners would collapse. If He released her, they could accuse Him of disregarding Scripture. Their attempt to stone her was not an expression of their holiness but a declaration of their hostility. They cared nothing for the woman's soul. Their only goal was to disgrace Jesus. Yet in trying to trap Him, they revealed their own hearts. They stood with stones in their hands but sin in their hearts, ready to condemn her while refusing to examine themselves.

Jesus answered their accusation with silence, stooping low and writing in the dust. The law demanded judgment, yet the Lawgiver Himself knelt in the dirt beside the guilty. When He finally spoke, His words carried both truth and grace: "He who is without sin among you, let him throw a stone at her first" (v. 7). With one sentence, He upheld the law's righteousness, exposed their hypocrisy, and dismantled their trap.

They had weaponized the law to condemn another while ignoring its voice when it confronted them. One by one, the stones fell. The courtroom emptied. Mercy triumphed over judgment (James 2:13).

This scene teaches us something vital for evangelism: The law is meant to reveal guilt, not to remove compassion. Jesus did not deny her sin, nor did He dismiss its seriousness. But He refused to let self-righteous people use the law as a shield to hide their own hearts. When we share the gospel, we must hold the same tension, letting God's Word expose sin without losing sight of the broken person standing before us. The law humbles, but grace heals. Evangelism requires both: truth that convicts and grace that restores.

Lifted by Grace

When the dust settled and the accusers disappeared, only two remained: the guilty and the guiltless. The woman stood waiting for the sentence she fully deserved. Jesus stood ready to give the mercy she never expected. "Woman, where are those accusers of yours? Has no one condemned you?"

(v. 10). She answered, "No one, Lord." Then Jesus spoke the words that have lifted countless souls from despair: "Neither do I condemn you; go and sin no more" (v. 11).

These words reveal the very balance every evangelist must learn. Jesus did not say, "Your sin doesn't matter." He held truth and grace together in perfect unity. He removed her condemnation—that is grace. He called her to leave her sin—that is truth. One without the other would distort the gospel. Grace without truth leaves people bound; truth without grace leaves them broken. Jesus offered both, and in doing so He showed the woman what new life looks like: forgiven, freed, and now called to walk in holiness. The law and the gospel are not enemies; they work together. The law brought her to Jesus' feet, but grace lifted her up from the dust.

For evangelism, this encounter teaches us that broken people rarely need us to explain their sin. They already feel its weight. What they need is someone who can speak truth with the tenderness of Jesus. "Neither do I condemn you" is not a dismissal of sin; it is an invitation to freedom. "Go and sin no more" is not a threat; it is the power of grace calling a life out of bondage. When we share the gospel, we must offer both: the honesty that reveals sin and the mercy that reveals the Savior.

Recognizing the Guilty and Condemned

The woman caught in adultery represents those who are painfully aware of their guilt and crushed under the weight of accusation. Their sin may be public, recent, or deeply shameful, and others may use their failures to condemn or expose them. These individuals often feel trapped, believing their sin defines them and that God's judgment is certain. Jesus shows that the guilty and accused do not need stones. They need mercy, truth, and the hope of a new beginning.

How to Recognize Them

These individuals can often be recognized by the way they:

- Speak openly about their failures because the guilt already feels overwhelming.
- Fear rejection and judgment from others.
- Carry deep regret over choices that have hurt themselves or others.
- Believe they have disqualified themselves from God's forgiveness.
- Avoid spiritual conversations because they expect condemnation.
- Identify themselves primarily by their sin or past mistakes.

How to Engage Them

When speaking with them, it is helpful to:

- Lead with compassion, recognizing their pain before addressing their sin.

- Remind them that Jesus knows the worst about them and still extends mercy.
- Share scriptures that highlight forgiveness, restoration, and God's compassion.
- Avoid harsh tones; these individuals have already heard enough condemnation.
- Help them separate who they are from what they have done.
- Present the gospel as an invitation to freedom, not a list of demands.
- Point them to Jesus' words: "Neither do I condemn you; go and sin no more."

What They Might Say

- "I've messed up too badly for God to forgive me."
- "Everyone knows what I've done."
- "I feel ashamed just walking into a church."
- "I deserve whatever punishment I get."
- "I know God must be disappointed in me."

Those who are condemned and ashamed need to hear that Jesus offers mercy without ignoring the truth. They must be shown that forgiveness and restoration begin not with condemnation but with the grace that lifts them from the dust.

Bringing It Home: Using This in Practice

When you meet a "condemned and ashamed" person—someone who feels exposed, broken, and certain that God wants nothing to do with them—remember how Jesus spoke to the woman caught in adultery. He didn't excuse her sin, but He didn't crush her with it either. He offered her mercy that lifted her and truth that freed her.

If someone says, "I've messed up too badly for God to forgive me."

You might respond, "There's a story where Jesus met a woman in that exact place. Can I show you what He said to her?"

This gently invites them to see themselves in her story without feeling judged.

If someone says, "I don't deserve a second chance."

You could say, "None of us do, and that's what makes grace so powerful. Jesus gives mercy to those who least expect it. Let me show you an example."

This affirms their honesty while pointing them toward hope.

If someone says, "God must be done with me."

You might reply, "That's exactly how the woman in John 8 felt, but Jesus didn't walk away from her. He lifted her up. Can I tell you how He responded?"

This shows that Jesus moves toward the fallen, not away from them.

Broken people don't need stones thrown at them; they

need a Savior who stoops low enough to lift them up. Truth reveals their need, and grace shows them where healing is found.

Key Verses to Remember

John 8:11 – *And Jesus said to her, "Neither do I condemn you; go and sin no more."*

- Grace removes condemnation; truth calls us into holiness.

Psalm 34:18 – *The Lord is near to those who have a broken heart, and saves such as have a contrite spirit.*

- God moves toward the broken, not away from them.

James 2:13 – *For judgment is without mercy to the one who has shown no mercy. Mercy triumphs over judgment.*

- Mercy reflects the character of God and reveals a heart humbled by grace.

Romans 8:1 – There is *therefore now no condemnation to those who are in Christ Jesus.*

- In Christ, forgiveness comes first; transformation follows.

Romans 5:20 – *But where sin abounded, grace abounded much more.*

- No sin outweighs the abundance of Christ's grace.

Principles for Today

- Grace meets people where sin has left them.
- We cannot lift anyone until we are willing to stoop beside them.
- Truth and grace must never be separated.
- Truth exposes the wound; grace applies the healing.
- Condemnation cannot change a heart.
- Only mercy can lead someone to repentance and new life.
- Jesus deals personally with the guilty.
- He does not excuse sin but never abandons the sinner who turns to Him.
- The gospel lifts what the law lays bare.
- The law reveals our need; grace restores what sin has broken.

Closing Thoughts

Jesus meets the guilty and accused with mercy that restores rather than condemns. His response teaches us to hold grace and truth together as we walk with those burdened by their past. This chapter calls you to speak hope into lives crushed by shame, reminding them that Christ offers forgiveness and a new beginning. As you share His compassion, trust that His grace reaches deeper than any sin. May you reflect His heart consistently, lifting broken lives from the dust and pointing them to the Savior who makes all things new.

Chapter 9

From Tombs to Testimony

Reaching the Outcast and Bound

Main Passage: Mark 5:1–20

Key Verse: *Go home to your friends, and tell them what great things the Lord has done for you, and how He has had compassion on you.* —Mark 5:19

A Man No One Could Tame

When Jesus stepped out of the boat into the country of the Gadarenes, a region across the Sea of Galilee, He was immediately met by a man whose life had descended into unbearable torment. He lived among the tombs—isolated, naked, scarred, crying out night and day. Chains could not restrain him, and no one dared come near. Family, friends, and community had given up hope. He was the person society avoids, the one people talk about but never talk to. He was feared, forgotten, and left to destroy himself among the dead.

This is what sin and Satan do. They isolate. They dehumanize. They strip a person of peace, belonging, and purpose. The Gadarene man is not just a story of ancient demon possession; he is a picture of spiritual bondage in every generation. Today the chains may look different: addiction, rage, trauma, shame, bitterness, or self-destructive habits. But the symptoms are the same: broken relationships, deep wounds, and lives that feel beyond repair.

And yet even in this chaos, the man ran toward Jesus. Before he ever understood who Christ was, desperation pulled him to the only One who could step into his darkness without fear. The townspeople saw a threat; Jesus saw a soul. The world heard screams; Jesus heard a cry for deliverance. This is where every true gospel encounter begins, not with a put-together person seeking answers but with a broken person in need of a Savior strong enough to step into the tombs of their life.

The Power That Crosses Boundaries

Jesus did not arrive among the Gadarenes by accident. The night before, He had led His disciples straight into a violent storm—a storm so fierce that seasoned fishermen feared for their lives. That storm wasn't merely weather; it was resistance. Darkness does not surrender territory quietly. Yet Jesus pressed on, crossed the sea, and placed His feet on ground no

Jew would willingly approach—a Gentile region filled with tombs and pigs.

Everything about the place shouted "unclean," but the gospel moves toward what others avoid. It crosses the lines of comfort, prejudice, and convenience to reach people others have written off.

The man who met Jesus there embodied everything society fearfully disregards. He was isolated, uncontrollable, and spiritually bound. No one could tame him, but Jesus didn't come to tame him; He came to transform him. Before a word was exchanged, the man ran toward Jesus and fell before Him. Even the demonic forces inside him recognized what the surrounding community had not: The Son of the Most High God had arrived, and His authority was unmatched.

For the evangelist, this moment is deeply instructive. Some of the people Jesus calls us to reach will not be neatly packaged or socially safe. They may be bound by addiction, trauma, rage, or despair. Their outward behavior may intimidate others, but beneath the turmoil is a person made in God's image—someone Christ cares enough to cross seas, storms, and social boundaries to reach. The power of the gospel does not wait for someone to become "reachable;" it reaches into the darkness and begins its work there.

A Cry and a Command

When the man ran to Jesus and fell before Him, the words that came out were not his own. They were the desperate protest of the spirits that controlled him. "What have I to do with You, Jesus, Son of the Most High God?" (v. 7). The world saw a man beyond hope; Jesus saw a man bound. While others focused on his violence, Jesus spoke directly to the darkness enslaving him: "Come out of the man, you unclean spirit!" (v. 8). The authority in His voice revealed what even the demons already knew: He was Lord over every realm, visible and invisible.

This moment reveals a truth essential for evangelism: People are not our enemies. Behind the brokenness we see—addiction, anger, rebellion, fear—there is a deeper spiritual battle waging within. The man's outward torment was only the surface of an inward bondage. His cry was the cry of someone desperate for deliverance, even if his chains made it impossible for him to articulate that desire.

Jesus responded not with fear, avoidance, or frustration, but with command and compassion. He confronted the real enemy while moving toward the captive with mercy. The demons begged Jesus for permission to enter the herd of pigs, revealing yet again His absolute authority. Everything bowed before Him—storms, spirits, and sin. For the evangelist, this teaches confidence. Our hope in reaching the outcast and oppressed is not our strategy but Christ's supremacy. We speak because He reigns. We move toward the broken because His light cannot be overcome. And we believe in transformation because no chain is greater than His command.

Freedom and Restoration

When the townspeople arrived, they were met with a sight they never imagined. The man who once raged among tombs now sat clothed, calm, and restored. The one they feared had been transformed. But instead of rejoicing, they were afraid. The miracle unsettled them. Jesus had delivered a man no one could tame, yet their focus was fixed on the herd of pigs that had been lost. The cost of his restoration felt too high. Rather than welcome the One who brought freedom, they begged Him to leave their region (v. 17).

This reaction is more common than we imagine. Some people become comfortable with brokenness around them because it does not disturb their routines. They fear the change Jesus brings, not because His power is unclear but because it is unmistakably disruptive. The gospel restores what sin destroys, but it also exposes what people prefer to keep hidden: priorities, idols, and the illusion of control. The same light that brought peace to the demoniac felt threatening to those whose hearts preferred the shadows.

For the evangelist, this moment teaches something essential: Not everyone celebrates the liberation of the oppressed. Sometimes the greatest resistance comes not from the bound person but from the bystanders—family members, friends, or entire communities who fear what transformation might reveal. When Jesus frees someone, the ripple effects reach far beyond one life. And not everyone greets freedom with faith.

Go and Tell

When the people begged Jesus to leave their region, the healed man begged to go with Him. But Jesus had a different mission for him: "Go home to your friends, and tell them what great things the Lord has done for you, and how He has had compassion on you" (v. 19). The first missionary to the Decapolis was not a rabbi or an apostle; it was a man restored from the brink of destruction.

Jesus didn't take him along; He sent him out. The man who once shouted in torment would now proclaim the praises of the One who called him out of darkness (1 Pet. 2:9). His scars became his sermon. His deliverance became his message. He had no training and no strategy—only a story of what Jesus had done. And that was enough.

The mission field Jesus gave him wasn't distant; it was local, relational, and familiar. Evangelism begins right where we are, among the people who can already see the difference Christ has made. Effective witness is not about eloquence but authenticity, showing what Jesus has done and how His mercy has rewritten your story.

For every believer, this encounter is a reminder that deliverance leads to declaration. Jesus rescues us so we can speak of His compassion. He restores us so we can reveal His grace. He frees us so we can point others to the same hope. No one is too broken for grace, and no story is too small for God to use.

Recognizing the Outcast and Bound

The man among the tombs represents those who live in deep spiritual bondage and inner turmoil. Their lives may appear chaotic, unstable, or marked by self-destructive patterns, yet beneath the brokenness is a desperate longing for freedom. These individuals often feel controlled by forces they cannot name or overcome. Jesus shows that even the most bound soul is within reach of His authority, compassion, and restoring power.

How to Recognize Them

These individuals can often be recognized by the way they:

- Exhibit patterns of addiction, destructive behavior, or bondage they can't break.
- Feel isolated or rejected because of their past or their struggles.
- Experience intense inner turmoil, fear, or spiritual confusion.
- Talk openly about darkness, oppression, or feeling controlled by sin.
- Cycle between wanting help and pushing others away.
- Believe they are too damaged or too far gone for God to heal or restore.

How to Engage Them

When speaking with them, it is helpful to:

- Approach them with patience and compassion, knowing their battles run deep.
- Emphasize Jesus' authority over sin, darkness, and spiritual bondage.
- Share stories or scripture that highlight Christ's power to set people free.
- Avoid minimizing their struggles—take them seriously and listen carefully.
- Point them gently to the hope, peace, and identity found only in Christ.
- Encourage next steps toward community, accountability, and discipleship.
- Assure them that transformation is possible, even when it feels impossible.

What They Might Say

- "Something has a hold on me, and I can't break free."
- "People don't understand what's going on inside me."
- "I feel like I've lost control of my life."
- "I'm tired of living like this, but I don't know how to change."
- "I feel trapped, like there's no way out."

Those who are outcast and bound need to see that Jesus is stronger than the chains that hold them. They must encounter the Savior who speaks peace to their torment, restores their identity, and sends them out with a testimony of His transforming power.

Bringing It Home: How to Use This in Practice

When you meet an "outcast and oppressed" person—someone living in cycles of fear, addiction, or hopelessness—remember how Jesus met the man among the tombs. He did not avoid him, fear him, or shame him. He crossed the sea, confronted the darkness, restored his dignity, and then sent him with a purpose. Evangelism among the broken begins with compassion but depends on the power of Christ.

If someone says, "I've ruined everything."

You might reply, "There was a man in the Bible who felt the same way, living among tombs, completely hopeless. Jesus crossed a stormy sea just to reach him. Can I show you what happened next?"

This helps them see that Jesus moves toward the hopeless, not away from them.

If they say, "I can't control it anymore."

You could say, "That's how the man in Mark 5 felt until he met Someone stronger than his chains. Can I share with you what happened?"

This points them to Christ's authority rather than their ability.

If they say, "I don't belong anywhere."

You can respond, "Neither did the man among the tombs—until Jesus restored him and gave him a purpose. Would you like to hear what happened?"

This shows that identity and belonging are found in Christ, not circumstances.

If someone says, "No one can help me."

You can respond, "That's exactly what people thought about the man among the tombs. But Jesus stepped right into his darkness and set him free."

This opens the door to show Christ's power to deliver.

Broken people don't need advice that manages their chains. They need hope that breaks them. Jesus still crosses boundaries to reach the unreachable, and He often sends us to carry that hope.

Key Verses to Remember

Mark 5:15 – *Then they came to Jesus, and saw the one* who had been *demon-possessed and had the legion, sitting and clothed and in his right mind.*

- The gospel not only frees but restores what sin and darkness have shattered.

Psalm 107:14 – *He brought them out of darkness and the shadow of death, and broke their chains in pieces.*

- No bondage is too strong for the saving power of God.

John 8:36 – *Therefore if the Son makes you free, you shall be free indeed.*

- True and lasting freedom is found only in Christ.

Ephesians 6:12 – *For we do not wrestle against flesh and blood, but against principalities, against powers.*

- Some bondage is spiritual in nature and cannot be overcome apart from Christ's authority.

Mark 5:19 – *Go home to your friends, and tell them what great things the Lord has done for you.*

- Every freed life becomes a testimony that points others to Christ.

Principles for Today

- The gospel goes where comfort won't.
- Jesus crosses boundaries we often avoid so the bound can be set free.
- No one is too broken for Christ to restore.
- The tombs that terrify others are the very places Jesus transforms.
- Deliverance reveals the authority of Christ.
- What chains cannot do, His word accomplishes instantly.
- Compassion and authority must work together.

- Love moves us toward the oppressed; Christ's power gives us confidence.
- Restored people become witnesses.
- Those freed by Christ are sent to declare the mercy that found them.

Closing Thoughts

Jesus demonstrates His authority over darkness as He frees the man bound by spiritual chains. His example shows us that no life is too broken for His restoring power. This chapter encourages you to approach the spiritually oppressed with courage, compassion, and prayerful dependence. As you speak hope to those who feel trapped, trust that Christ can bring peace where there has been torment, and freedom where there has been bondage. May you boldly share the gospel, believing that every testimony of deliverance begins with the Savior's mighty word.

Chapter 10

Faith for the Skeptic

Reaching the Doubting and Uncertain

Main Passage: John 20:24–29

Key Verse: *Blessed* are *those who have not seen and* yet *have believed.* —John 20:29

A Disciple Missing in Action

Thomas wasn't with the other disciples when Jesus first appeared after the resurrection. Scripture doesn't explain why, but the clues are strong: grief, disappointment, and confusion likely pushed him into isolation. The Lord he trusted had been crucified, and the world he expected had collapsed. When hope feels shattered, retreat often feels safer than community. Many who wrestle with doubt today do the same. They pull back from fellowship, prayer, and truth at the very moment they need them most.

But notice this: Jesus did not scold Thomas for being absent. He didn't write him off, overlook him, or leave him behind. He went looking for him. This is a critical lesson for evangelism. Not everyone who drifts is rebellious; some are simply heartbroken. Behind many skeptical statements is a wounded soul trying to make sense of pain. Doubt often springs from disappointment, not defiance. Before we speak to the mind of a skeptic, we must learn to listen for the ache of their heart.

Evangelism sometimes begins not with answers but with presence—showing up, staying near, and refusing to let someone's absence become a barrier to Jesus' presence. Thomas missed the first meeting, but Jesus made sure he didn't miss the second.

Honest Doubt, Not Hostile Rebellion

Thomas is often remembered by a nickname Scripture never gives him: "Doubting Thomas." But his doubt wasn't the aggressive unbelief of a hardened heart; it was the ache of a wounded disciple. His world had been shaken. His hopes had died on a cross. And now the others claimed to have seen Jesus alive. Thomas wasn't rejecting Christ; he was struggling to believe again after crushing disappointment. His words, "Unless I see . . . I will not believe" (v. 25), were not defiance but longing.

Jesus never shamed sincere wrestlers. Scripture says, "Be merciful to those who doubt" (Jude 22, NIV). The patience

Jesus showed Thomas is the same patience He extends to countless skeptics today. Many who push back aren't trying to rebel; they're trying to reconcile their pain with their faith. Beneath the questions is a heart that wants to believe but feels unable to.

For evangelism, this is crucial. Doubt is not the enemy; despair is. Our job is not to scold the skeptic but to gently guide them toward the Savior. Instead of treating uncertainty as rejection, we approach it as an open door. Jesus didn't crush Thomas; He invited him closer. So must we.

When Jesus Meets the Skeptic

Eight days passed before Jesus appeared again. That detail matters. Jesus did not rush the process or pressure Thomas into belief. He gave him space to wrestle, grieve, and think, but He didn't leave him in his uncertainty.

This time Thomas was present, and Jesus came straight to him. He didn't begin with rebuke but with invitation: "Reach your finger here . . . reach your hand *here* . . . do not be unbelieving, but believing" (v. 27).

Jesus met Thomas at the precise point of his struggle. He addressed the very conditions Thomas himself had set: "Unless I see . . . unless I touch." Jesus didn't need Thomas to touch His wounds. Thomas needed it.

And notice this: Jesus offered evidence, but He also called for surrender. He didn't only say, "See," but He said, "Believe." The purpose of meeting Thomas's need wasn't to win an argument; it was to win his heart. Evangelism isn't about giving every answer a skeptic demands; it's about guiding them to the moment where the risen Christ calls them to trust. Jesus brought truth near and invited Thomas to step toward Him in faith.

This is the pattern we follow. We listen, we understand, we walk patiently. Then we point clearly to Christ. Skeptics do not need us to prove everything. They need us to faithfully bring them to the One who can open their eyes.

From Proof to Surrender

When Thomas finally stood face to face with the risen Christ, everything shifted. Jesus offered the very evidence Thomas had demanded, yet what transformed him wasn't the sight of the wounds. It was the presence of the One who bore them. The resurrected Lord didn't simply answer his questions; He invited Thomas to trust again.

Thomas's response was immediate and overwhelming: "My Lord and my God!" (v. 28). In one breath, the disciple who struggled to believe became the first to explicitly confess Jesus' full deity. Proof opened the door, but encounter brought him to his knees. This is the aim of every gospel conversation—not merely to provide evidence but to lead people to the living Christ who alone can turn doubt into devotion.

Jesus then spoke words meant not only for Thomas but for every generation after him: "Blessed *are* those who have not seen and *yet* have believed" (v. 29). Faith is not blind; it rests on trustworthy testimony. But it also moves beyond sight into surrender. We have never touched His scars or heard His physical voice, yet we behold Him through the Scriptures He has given and the Spirit who opens our eyes. Evangelism helps doubters take that same step—from demanding proof to meeting a Person, from investigation to worship.

Recognizing the Doubting and Uncertain

Thomas represents those who struggle to believe unless they can see or verify truth for themselves. Their skepticism does not come from hostility but from unmet expectations, past disappointments, or a desire for certainty. These individuals often wrestle with doubts quietly, fearing judgment for their questions. Jesus shows that honest doubters are not cast aside. He meets them where they are and invites them to move from uncertainty to confident faith.

How to Recognize Them

These individuals can often be recognized by the way they:

- Express hesitation to believe without evidence or personal experience.
- Ask sincere but challenging questions about faith, Scripture, or the gospel.

- Wrestle with disappointment, unanswered prayers, or unmet expectations.
- Fear being judged for their doubts, so they hide them behind silent sarcasm.
- Struggle to trust God because of past hurts or experiences with unreliable people.
- Want to believe but feel stuck between desire and uncertainty.

How to Engage Them

When speaking with them, it is helpful to:

- Welcome their questions without shaming or dismissing them.
- Ask what specifically makes believing difficult for them.
- Share how Jesus responded gently to Thomas's doubts.
- Point them to scriptures that highlight God's faithfulness and patience.
- Encourage them to take small steps of trust.
- Highlight evidence of Christ's resurrection in a simple and personal way.
- Remind them that faith is not the absence of questions but the presence of trust in Christ.

What They Might Say

- "I want to believe, but I need more proof."
- "Why would God let that happen?"
- "I've prayed before and nothing changed."
- "I have too many questions about the Bible."
- "I'm just not sure I can believe what I can't see."
- "If God is real, why doesn't He show Himself?"

Those who are skeptical and doubting need patience, not pressure. They must encounter the Savior who meets them in their questions and gently leads them toward a faith grounded in His presence and truth.

Bringing It Home: Using This in Practice

When you meet a "Thomas"—someone wrestling with doubt, confusion, or disappointment—remember how Jesus met Thomas: patiently, personally, and without shame. Doubters don't need pressure; they need presence. Evangelism among the uncertain begins with listening, offering scripture gently, and inviting them to consider Jesus again rather than demanding instant belief.

If someone says, "I just can't believe unless I see proof."

You could respond: "Thomas felt the same way, but Jesus met him right in the middle of those questions. Can I show you how He did it?"

This helps them see that Jesus does not reject honest doubt but responds to it.

If someone says, "I used to believe, but too much has happened."

You might say: "Thomas' hope collapsed too—until Jesus showed up again. Can I share that moment with you?"

This shows that disappointment can be a doorway for Christ to reveal Himself.

If someone says, "Why doesn't God just show Himself?"

You can reply: "Jesus told Thomas that those who believe without seeing are blessed, and He gives us His Word so we can see Him. Would you read His story with me?"

This gently points them to Scripture as the place where Christ reveals Himself.

If someone says, "I have too many questions to be a Christian."

You can say: "Questions didn't push Jesus away from Thomas; they brought Him closer. Would you be open to exploring those questions together?"

This opens space for honest conversation rather than debate.

Doubters don't need an argument; they need an invitation. Patient, steady presence—grounded in Scripture—can lead them from uncertainty to worship.

Key Verses to Remember

John 20:29 – *Blessed* are *those who have not seen and* yet *have believed.*

- Jesus honors faith that trusts His Word even when sight is absent.

Jude 22 (NIV) – *Be merciful to those who doubt.*

- Doubters need patient mercy, not pressure or shame.

Romans 10:17 – *So then faith* comes *by hearing, and hearing by the word of God.*

- The path from doubt to belief is shaped by Scripture.

Mark 9:24 – *Lord, I believe; help my unbelief!*

- Jesus meets honest doubt with grace, not condemnation.

Hebrews 11:1 – *Now faith is the substance of things hoped for, the evidence of things not seen.*

- True faith anchors itself in God's promises, not visible proof.

Principles for Today

- Doubt is often rooted in pain, not rebellion.
- Behind many questions is a wounded heart longing for reassurance.
- Jesus meets honest doubters with patience and grace.
- He does not rush or shame those who struggle; He invites them to trust again.
- Faith is strengthened through encounter with Christ.
- Evidence may open the door, but only Christ brings someone to faith.
- The Word of God reveals the risen Christ to every generation.
- We help the doubting by opening the Scriptures that testify of Jesus.
- Believers are called to walk with those who wrestle with uncertainty.
- Gentle questions and patient friendship create space for faith to awaken.

Closing Thoughts

Jesus meets honest doubt with patience and clarity, inviting Thomas to move from uncertainty to faith. His example teaches us to welcome questions and guide the skeptical with humility and grace. This chapter encourages you to honor the sincerity of those who wrestle with belief. As you walk beside them, trust the Spirit to reveal truth and deepen their faith. May you speak with gentleness, confident that Christ still meets doubting hearts and leads them to the joy of believing.

Chapter 11

Called from the Branches

Reaching the Curious and Seeking

Main Passage: Luke 19:1–10

Key Verse: *For the Son of Man has come to seek and to save that which was lost.* —Luke 19:10

A Curious Climb

Zacchaeus did not wake up that morning expecting a transformed life. He was not seeking forgiveness, clarity, or spiritual renewal. He was simply curious. Word of Jesus had spread, and as the crowd pressed through Jericho's narrow streets, something in Zacchaeus stirred—a whisper of longing, a pull he could not explain. He wanted "to see who Jesus was" (v. 3). It was not yet faith, not yet conviction—just curiosity. But curiosity is often the first step toward grace.

Blocked by both his height and the hostility of the crowd, Zacchaeus did something no wealthy official would normally do. He ran ahead and climbed a sycamore tree. The chief tax collector, who had spent years taking from others, now perched above the masses, looking down at the One he hoped to glimpse. Pride took a back seat to desire. Dignity bowed to hunger. This is how many people begin their spiritual journey. Before conviction comes curiosity. Before repentance comes interest. Before surrender comes a longing to look.

Evangelism often begins here, with the heart that is leaning in, not fully understanding but unable to turn away. Zacchaeus climbed to see Jesus, but his curiosity was not self-generated. It was the early evidence of God's drawing, a gentle pull toward the Savior he had never met.

A Savior Who Sees and Calls

Zacchaeus climbed the tree to catch a glimpse of Jesus, but Jesus stopped beneath the branches and looked up at him. This is grace: the One who seeks the lost standing beneath the limbs where a seeker sits. Before Zacchaeus said a word, Jesus called him by name: "Zacchaeus, make haste and come down, for today I must stay at your house" (v. 5).

His words reveal the heart of Christ:

- Personal – He calls Zacchaeus by name.
- Urgent – "Make haste."

- Purposeful – "I must stay."
- Relational – "At your house."

The crowd grumbled. They saw a traitor, a thief, a man whose wealth was soaked in the suffering of others. But Jesus saw someone being drawn by the Father. Curious people are often weighed down by the judgments of others, yet Jesus walks straight toward them with compassion and invitation.

Zacchaeus "made haste" and "received Him joyfully" (v. 6). The spark of curiosity ignited into readiness. A seeking sinner had been found by a seeking Savior.

A Repentance That Looks Like Restoration

Between verses 7 and 8, something happened—unwritten but undeniable. The grace that called Zacchaeus from the tree now awakened repentance in his heart. Standing before the Lord, he declared, "Look, Lord, I give half my goods to the poor; and if I have taken anything from anyone by false accusation, I restore fourfold" (v. 8).

Jesus never commanded this. He never lectured him on greed, integrity, or restitution. Zacchaeus's change was the natural overflow of a heart awakened by grace. What the law could not produce through pressure, grace produced through presence. Repentance is not a payment for sins but the evidence of a transformed heart.

Jesus affirmed it: "Today salvation has come to this house . . . for the Son of Man has come to seek and to save that which was lost" (vv. 9–10). Zacchaeus was not saved because of what he gave but because of the One he received.

This is the pattern of seekers:

> curiosity → encounter → invitation → surrender → transformation

Evangelism requires patience, discernment, and the recognition that God often works long before a person realizes what is happening inside them.

The Mission Defined

Jesus ends the encounter with one of the clearest mission statements in all of Scripture: "For the Son of Man has come to seek and to save that which was lost" (v. 10). Zacchaeus wasn't saved because he climbed a tree. He was saved because Jesus came seeking him. His curiosity was the doorway through which divine pursuit entered.

Recognizing the Curious and Drawn

Zacchaeus represents those whose hearts are beginning to stir, people who may not fully understand what they're seeking yet feel drawn to look closer. They are not resistant or argumentative; they are open, attentive, and quietly searching. Something in them is awakening, and they begin positioning themselves near truth, listening from a distance, or asking early questions. Their curiosity is sincere, though still forming. This gentle openness often marks the first steps of a heart being drawn toward Christ.

How to Recognize Them

These individuals can often be recognized by the way they:

- Show sudden interest in spiritual things.
- Ask exploratory questions without argument.
- Express longing, emptiness, or curiosity.
- Begin attending or watching church from a distancc.
- Describe a sense of "something drawing them."
- Position themselves near Christians without fully engaging them.
- Speak about God with openness rather than skepticism.

How to Engage Them

When speaking with them, it is helpful to:

- Affirm their interest without pressuring them.
- Ask gentle questions that draw out what God is already stirring.
- Focus on who Jesus is, not on what they must do next.

- Share simple truths that feed their interest without overwhelming them.
- Reflect Christ's kindness in your tone and presence.
- Offer next steps, not full expectations.
- Be patient; curiosity often matures slowly into conviction.

What They Might Say

- "I've been thinking more about God lately."
- "I'm not religious, but I'm searching."
- "I started reading the Bible."
- "I've been watching church online."
- "I feel like something is missing."
- "I don't know why, but I feel drawn."

These statements are the spiritual equivalent of Zacchaeus climbing a tree. They're looking from the branches. They're watching from a distance. They are open, waiting for someone who notices them.

Bringing It Home: Using This in Practice

When you meet a "Zacchaeus"—someone curious and watching from a distance—it's important to remember that curiosity is often the first sign of a heart beginning to open. These individuals may not be ready for deep conversation, but they are willing to look closer and take small steps toward truth. Your role is to guide them gently, noticing their interest and helping them move forward without pressure or being overwhelmed.

If someone says, "I've been reading about Jesus lately."

You could respond: "That's wonderful. What sparked your interest?"

This invites them to share the story behind their curiosity.

If someone says, "I don't know what I believe, but I'm searching."

You might say: "Jesus welcomes honest seekers. Could we look at one of His encounters together?"

This gently moves them toward Scripture.

If someone says, "I'm not ready for church, but I want to learn more."

You can reply: "Let's take it a step at a time. What's on your mind?"

This validates their pace while offering guidance.

If someone says, "I'm looking for hope, but I don't know where to start."

You can say: "Let's start with who Jesus is. That's where Zacchaeus began, and Jesus met him right where he was."

This helps them see that hope begins not with perfect understanding but with a simple, honest, step toward Christ.

Seekers don't need pressure; they need patient, thoughtful guidance from someone who sees what Jesus sees.

Key Verses to Remember

Luke 19:10 – *For the Son of Man has come to seek and to save that which was lost.*

- Jesus pursues seekers long before they pursue Him.

John 6:44 – *No one can come to Me unless the Father who sent Me draws him.*

- Curiosity is often evidence of divine drawing.

Jeremiah 29:13 – *And you will seek Me and find* Me, *when you search for Me with all your heart.*

- God promises to reveal Himself to those who genuinely seek Him.

Isaiah 55:6 – *Seek the Lord while He may be found, call upon Him while He is near.*

- The invitation is urgent; respond while grace is near.

Hebrews 11:6 – *He is a rewarder of those who diligently seek Him.*

- God delights to meet those who move toward Him in faith.

Principles for Today

- Curiosity is often the first sign of God's drawing.
- The Spirit often stirs the heart before understanding develops.
- Jesus notices the seeker hidden in the crowd.
- He sees what others overlook: the quiet heart leaning toward truth.
- Grace invites before it confronts.
- Jesus meets seekers with kindness that leads them toward repentance.
- True seeking leads to genuine surrender.
- When Christ enters a life, repentance and transformation follow.
- Our role is to guide, not to pressure.
- We walk patiently with seekers as God continues His work within them.

Closing Thoughts

The encounter between Jesus and Zacchaeus reminds us that God often begins His work in the quiet stirrings of curiosity. Many people are not ready for deep discussion or dramatic decisions. They are simply taking early steps toward truth. This chapter teaches us to recognize those moments, respond with patience, and guide seekers gently toward Christ. As we sow the Word faithfully, we trust that the same Savior who called Zacchaeus by name is still drawing hearts today, inviting the curious to come down from the branches and experience the joy of His transforming grace.

Chapter 12

A Cry for Mercy

Guiding the Sinner's Response to the Gospel

Main Passages: Luke 15:11–24; 18:9–14; 23:39–43; Rom. 10:13

Key Verse: *Whoever calls on the name of the Lord shall be saved.* —Rom. 10:13

When the Heart Awakens

There are moments in evangelism when a person suddenly becomes deeply aware of their need for God. The Spirit has been working beneath the surface—softening, stirring, revealing, awakening. They may not know how to articulate it, but something inside them whispers, "I need to be made right with God."

This moment is sacred. It is not emotional hype or human

persuasion. It is not pressure, performance, or manipulation. It is the Spirit of God calling a sinner to Christ. Our role is not to control the moment but to honor it. We listen. We stay steady. We lift their eyes to Christ. And we guide them gently.

Salvation does not come because someone says the right words. Salvation comes when a sinner cries out to God in faith.

Why Words Alone Cannot Save

Many of us grew up hearing the "Sinner's Prayer." The words themselves are fine. Scripture is full of people calling on God. The danger is when prayer becomes a formula as if repeating a phrase guarantees salvation.

Scripture never instructs us to:

- Recite a specific sentence.
- Repeat words after someone.
- Trust in the prayer itself.

Jesus warned, "Not everyone who says to Me, 'Lord, Lord,' shall enter the kingdom of heaven" (Matt. 7:21). Right words alone are not enough. A surrendered heart is essential.

Then comes the promise: "Whoever calls upon the name of the Lord shall be saved" (Rom. 10:13). The call is not a ritual; it is an appeal for mercy. It is honesty, humility, and dependence. Salvation rests not in the prayer spoken but in the Savior who answers.

When the Heart Turns to God

Before any words are spoken, repentance begins inside. Scripture shows again and again that salvation isn't about getting the phrasing right. It's about turning toward God in trust and humility.

The Tax Collector (Luke 18:9–14)

He made no excuses, offered no defense. He stood afar off, unable to lift his eyes. His posture revealed repentance before his words did. His prayer was simple: "God, be merciful to me, a sinner!" (v. 13). No performance. No polish. Just honest need. Jesus said this man went home justified (v. 14). Repentance begins when we cast ourselves on God's mercy.

The Prodigal Son (Luke 15:11–24)

His repentance began in the far country when he realized the emptiness of his rebellion. He turned his steps toward home before he spoke a word. When he reached his father, he confessed: "Father, I have sinned against heaven and in your sight" (v. 21). No bargaining. No minimizing. He owned his sin and returned. Before he finished, the father ran to him, embraced him, and restored him. Repentance begins when we turn toward the Father, even while our words are imperfect or unfinished.

The Thief on the Cross (Luke 23:39–43)

He didn't defend himself. "We indeed justly," he said, acknowledging his guilt (v. 41). He confessed Christ's innocence: "This Man has done nothing wrong" (v. 41). Then he confessed Christ's authority: "Lord, remember me when You come into Your kingdom" (v. 42). No promises, no religious ceremony. Just faith calling out to the Savior. Jesus replied, "Today you will be with Me in Paradise" (v. 43). Repentance begins when we trust Christ alone with nothing to bring but need.

Recognizing the Repentant

Some individuals reach a point where the Spirit has already done the heavy lifting. Their hearts are softened, their defenses are lowered, and their need for grace is apparent. They are not resisting, arguing, or hiding anymore. They are seeking. This is the moment every evangelist must learn to recognize. When a heart is repentant and ready, your role is not to pressure or persuade, but to guide them gently toward the Savior who is already drawing them.

How to Recognize Them

These individuals can often be recognized by the way they:

- Admit their sin honestly without excuses or self-justification.

- Express a real desire to change and be made right with God.
- Ask questions that reveal conviction rather than resistance.
- Show humility rather than defensiveness.
- Speak with sincerity rather than debate or distraction.
- Demonstrate a soft, tender heart that is open to truth.

How to Engage Them

When speaking with them, it is helpful to:

- Slow down and let the Spirit continue His work. Don't rush the moment.
- Affirm what God is already awakening in their heart.
- Use clear, simple scripture to show how sinners come to Christ.
- Emphasize repentance, faith, and surrender rather than formulas or phrases.
- Invite them to speak to God in their own words instead of repeating yours.
- Reassure them that salvation rests on Christ, not on the perfection of their prayer.

What They Might Say

- "I know I need to give my life to Jesus."
- "I'm tired of running."
- "I just want to be forgiven."
- "I want to follow Him."

Those who are seeking and repentant need gentle guidance, not pressure. The Spirit has already opened their heart. Your role is simply to help them respond to Christ with sincerity, humility, and faith.

Bringing it Home: Using This in Practice

Moments like these are sacred. When someone is ready to trust Christ, you are standing on holy ground where eternity hangs in the balance and the Spirit is actively drawing a soul to salvation. Your task is not to manufacture conviction or manipulate emotion but to walk beside the person as God leads them to repentance and faith. Make sure they understand the gospel clearly. Let them confess honestly. Encourage them to pray in their own words. And remind them that salvation rests not in a repetition of phrases but in a heart that turns to Christ in surrender and trust.

Never rush someone into praying, and never pressure them. If their heart is ready, God will give them the words. If their heart is not ready, no words will save them. Guide humbly, speak clearly, and trust the Spirit completely, because in moments like these, He is the One who is doing the saving.

Key Verses to Remember

Romans 10:13 – *For whoever calls on the name of the Lord shall be saved.*

- Salvation is a sincere cry for mercy, not a recited formula.

Psalm 51:17 – *The sacrifices of God* are *a broken spirit, a broken and a contrite heart.*

- God responds to honest humility.

Luke 18:13 – *God, be merciful to me a sinner!*

- The simplest prayer of repentance is the truest.

Romans 10:9 – *If you confess with your mouth the Lord Jesus and believe in your heart that God has raised Him from the dead, you will be saved.*

- Salvation is believing and surrendering, not performing.

Psalm 86:5 – *For You, Lord,* are *good, and ready to forgive, and abundant in mercy to all those who call upon You.*

- We call upon Him because He is merciful and willing to forgive.

Principles for Today

- The Spirit—not us—awakens the heart.
- We guide, but God draws.
- Prayer is not a formula.
- Salvation is a heart cry to Christ, not perfect phrasing.
- Repentance begins with honesty.
- We come to God as we are, not as we wish to appear.
- Our role is to walk gently with those who are turning to Him.
- The moment belongs to the Spirit and the sinner—not the evangelist.

Closing Thoughts

Jesus shows that genuine repentance is a matter of the heart, not the repetition of a prayer. His approach teaches us to guide with clarity, patience, and deep dependence on the Spirit's work. This chapter calls you to honor the sacredness of leading someone to Christ by avoiding pressure and embracing humility. As you help others respond to the gospel, trust that God is drawing them with His kindness. May you walk forward with reverence, pointing repentant hearts to the Savior who receives all who come to Him in truth.

Conclusion

WALKING IN THE WAY OF THE MASTER

Following in His Footsteps

Jesus did not leave His followers to wonder how to carry His message into the world. He showed them. Chapter after chapter, passage after passage, we have watched Him meet people in their confusion, pride, pain, sin, and unbelief. He moved toward the religious and the rebellious, the self-assured and the self-condemned, the skeptic, the seeker, and the spiritually oppressed. Every encounter revealed something about His heart—and something about our mission.

Evangelism is not a program, a personality type, or a polished argument. It is the overflow of walking with Jesus. The more we see His compassion, the more we extend compassion. The more we trust His power, the more boldly we speak. The more we experience His mercy, the more eager we are to share it with those still searching for hope. His method shapes our method. His posture shapes our posture. His presence empowers our witness.

The Journey You Have Begun

If you have worked through these chapters slowly, honestly, and prayerfully, you have already taken significant steps toward becoming a faithful witness. You have looked at evangelism not as a task to perform but as a calling to embody. You have seen how Jesus spoke truth without arrogance, showed mercy without compromise, confronted hearts without crushing them, and offered grace without ignoring sin.

But learning these truths is only the beginning. Evangelism matures through practice—small steps, daily faithfulness, intentional conversations, and quiet obedience. As you step into your own encounters, the Spirit of God will remind you of what He has taught through His Word (John 16:26). You will see moments you once overlooked and recognize opportunities you once feared. The Master is still teaching His disciples, not from the shores of Galilee but through the testimonies of Scripture and the power of His Spirit.

Your Role in God's Mission

No believer is exempt from the Great Commission, and no believer is alone in it. God goes before you, the Spirit goes with you, and the gospel remains "the power of God to salvation" (Rom. 1:16). You are not responsible for changing hearts, only for planting and watering with faithfulness. Christ still transforms the proud like Nicodemus, the broken like the Samaritan woman, the guilty like the adulterous woman, the bound like the Gadarene, the self-justifying like the lawyer, and the doubting like Thomas.

Your life may never lead a crowd, but it can lead a soul to Christ. You may never preach a sermon, but you can speak a word of hope. You may feel ordinary, but God delights to use ordinary people who depend on Him.

Go in the Strength of the Lord

As this book closes, something else opens: your mission field. It includes your home, your church, your workplace, your neighborhood, and every relationship God has woven into your life. The stories you have studied are not simply ancient events; they are patterns for the Spirit's work today.

Walk with Jesus. Watch where He leads. Listen for the Spirit's prompting. Step into conversations with gentleness and truth. And trust that the One who transformed lives then is still transforming lives now.

The gospel does not need better methods; it needs faithful messengers.

May you become one.

PART 3

EQUIPPING FOR THE MISSION

Tools and Truths for Sharing the Gospel

Appendix A

YOUR STORY, HIS GLORY

Sharing Your Testimony with Scripture and Clarity

Why Your Story Matters

One of the simplest and most powerful evangelistic tools you have is your personal testimony. You do not need formal training or polished speaking ability to tell someone what Jesus has done for you. In fact, few things pierce the heart like a genuine story of grace. When Jesus delivered the demon-possessed man in Mark 5, He did not send him to seminary. He said, "Go home to your friends, and tell them what great things the Lord has done for you, and how He has had compassion on you" (Mark 5:19).

That is the essence of a testimony: declaring the Lord's compassion in your own life. You are not the hero; Christ is. When you share your story, you are not promoting yourself. You are pointing others to the mercy and power of Christ.

The Purpose of a Testimony

A testimony is not your life story. It is a living illustration of the gospel. When spoken clearly, it highlights three truths:

1. Who you were without Christ—lost and unable to save yourself.
2. How Christ drew you—through the Word, conviction, and grace.
3. Who you are now in Him—forgiven, changed, and growing.

This is how Paul shared his story (see Acts 22 and 26). Every time, his testimony:

- Began with honest confession.
- Centered on the death and resurrection of Jesus.
- Concluded with a changed direction.

Your testimony should lead to the gospel, not replace it.

A Clear and Simple Structure

Most testimonies can be shared in three to five minutes when needed. Clarity matters more than length.

Before Christ – My Need

- What shaped your identity?
- What were you trusting in?
- What was missing?

"All we like sheep have gone astray" (Isa. 53:6).

Keep this section brief and honest. Do not glorify sin. Highlight emptiness and need.

How Christ Drew Me – God's Work

- What truth confronted you?
- How did God open your eyes?
- What led you to call upon Him for mercy?

"Christ Jesus came into the world to save sinners" (1 Tim. 1:15).

If you prayed, focus on why you prayed, not merely that you prayed. The emphasis is on Christ's saving work, not your words.

Life After Christ – New Direction

- What has changed in your desires, peace, or purpose?

- What new relationship do you have with God?
- How is grace shaping you today?

"If anyone *is* in Christ, *he is* a new creation" (2 Cor. 5:17).

Be honest about ongoing growth, but highlight new direction, not perfection.

Weaving Scripture into Your Story

Sharing scripture with your testimony gives weight and clarity. Your experience is meaningful, but God's Word carries power.

Example connections:

Part of Testimony	Scripture to Anchor
Conviction of sin	Romans 3:23
Jesus' saving work	John 3:16; Acts 16:31
Forgiveness and cleansing	1 John 1:9
New life in Christ	2 Corinthians 5:17; Galatians 2:20

Your story becomes most powerful when it echoes God's Word. People may disagree with your experience, but they cannot overturn Scripture.

Practical Tips

- ***Keep Christ Central***

  Your story is a window. Let people see Him through it.

- ***Be Clear and Simple***

  Avoid Christian jargon or insider language.

- ***Be Honest***

  Authenticity speaks louder than dramatic detail.

- ***Be Prepared***

  Write and practice your testimony so it feels natural and sincere.

- ***Be Prayerful***

  Ask the Holy Spirit to lead you to the right moment and the right part of your story.

  "The Spirit . . . will testify of Me. And you also will bear witness" (John 15:26–27).

Putting It into Practice

Take time to write your testimony under these headings:

1. Before Christ: What was missing or broken?
2. How Christ Drew You: What truth changed your heart?
3. Life with Christ: What newness has He brought?

After you write it:

1. Look for ways to anchor each section in scripture.
2. Condense it into a short version you can share conversationally.
3. Ask God, "Who needs to hear how You have had compassion on me?"

You are not performing. You are bearing witness.

Closing Encouragement

Every believer's story is a miracle of mercy. Some were rescued from rebellion and others from self-righteousness, but all were rescued by grace. Your testimony is proof that the same Savior who found you is still pursuing others.

Tell your story—for His glory.

Appendix B

Answering Hard Questions

Responding to Doubts with Truth and Grace

Why Apologetics Matters

The word *apologetics* comes from the Greek *apologia*, which means "a reasoned defense." Peter wrote, "Always *be* ready to *give* a defense to everyone who asks you a reason for the hope that is in you, with meekness and fear" (1 Pet. 3:15). Apologetics is not about winning arguments; it is about removing obstacles that keep people from seeing Christ clearly. When we answer with both truth and tenderness, our defense becomes an invitation, not a confrontation.

Yet we must remember that no heart is changed by logic alone. Conviction and conversion belong to the Spirit. Our task is to speak faithfully, not forcefully. Truth offered in love gives the Spirit room to work.

Preparing Your Heart and Mind

Before speaking for Christ, spend time with Christ. Confidence comes from communion. Ask God to make you humble, patient, and discerning. Stay rooted in Scripture, the only weapon that pierces the heart (Heb. 4:12). If you don't know an answer, say so. Honesty builds credibility. Promise to search the Scriptures and follow through.

And above all, listen. Proverbs warns, "He who answers a matter before he hears *it*, it *is* folly and shame to him" (Prov. 18:13). Most objections carry wounds underneath such as confusion, disappointment, or betrayal. Listening reveals what needs healing.

1. How Can We Know God Exists?

Key Scriptures: Rom. 1:19–21; Ps. 19:1–4; Ps. 14:1; Acts 17:24–27; Col. 1:15–17

Everywhere we look, creation proclaims its Creator. The design, order, and beauty of the world bear unmistakable witness to an intelligent, purposeful mind behind it all. Paul wrote, "Since the creation of the world His invisible *attributes* are clearly seen . . . so that they are without excuse" (Rom. 1:20). No one will stand before God and truthfully say, "I didn't know."

David echoed the same truth: "The heavens declare the glory of God; and the firmament shows His handiwork" (Ps. 19:1). Creation does not whisper. It shouts. Every sunrise, every cell, every star is a sermon without words.

We instinctively recognize design. If you saw a building, you would never conclude it built itself. The same is true for DNA, cosmic order, and the complexity of life. To believe everything came from nothing requires more blind faith than to believe in God. "The fool has said in his heart, '*There is* no God'" (Ps. 14:1).

Creation isn't God's only witness. He placed another inside us: the conscience. Every culture recognizes moral laws because the Lawgiver has written His standards on the human heart (Rom. 2:15).

And finally, God has given the clearest revelation of all—Christ Himself. "He is the image of the invisible God" (Col. 1:15). Creation and conscience reveal that God exists; Jesus reveals who He is.

2. If God Is Good, Why Does He Allow Suffering?

Key Scriptures: Gen. 1:31; Gen. 3:16–19; Rom. 8:18–23; James 1:2–4; Rev. 21:4; 2 Pet. 3:13

God created a world without pain, death, or decay (Gen. 1:31). But when sin entered, everything broke. Humanity's rebellion fractured both the human heart and the created order. Paul wrote, "The whole creation groans" (Rom. 8:22), and we hear that groaning in storms, sickness, sorrow, and death.

Suffering is the ripple effect of the fall. Yet even in the brokenness, God's goodness shines. He did not remain distant; He entered the pain Himself. On the cross, Jesus bore the full weight of sin and its curse so He could redeem all who trust Him.

For believers, suffering is not punishment; it is preparation. “The sufferings of this present time are not worthy *to be compared* with the glory” to come (Rom. 8:18). Trials refine faith, deepen dependence, and produce endurance (James 1:2–4).

And this hope is certain: God will one day wipe away every tear (Rev. 21:4) and renew creation itself (2 Pet. 3:13). The world that groans today will one day be restored.

3. Is Jesus Really the Only Way?

Key Scriptures: John 14:6; Acts 4:12; 1 Tim. 2:5–6; John 3:16–18; Rom. 5:8–9

Jesus’ words in John 14:6 leave no ambiguity: “I am the way, the truth, and the life. No one comes to the Father except through Me.” If He truly rose from the dead, His claim stands above every philosophy and religion.

Christianity is exclusive in truth but inclusive in invitation. The door is narrow, but open to all.

Jesus is the only way because:

- ***Only He addressed the real problem: sin.***

  Religion offers advice; Christ offers rescue.

- ***Only He lived a sinless life and died in our place.***

  “It is finished” (John 19:30).

- ***Only He bridges the gap between God and man.***

  "One Mediator . . . *the* Man Christ Jesus" (1 Tim. 2:5).

God's love is not diminished by this exclusivity. It's proved by it (John 3:16). Jesus isn't one of many ways; He is God's way.

4. Is the Bible Trustworthy?

Key Scriptures: 2 Tim. 3:16–17; 2 Pet. 1:20–21; Ps. 12:6; John 10:35; Isa. 40:8

The Bible is unlike any other book—written by more than forty authors over fifteen centuries yet unified in theme, purpose, and message. Such harmony is evidence of a single divine Author.

"All Scripture *is* given by inspiration of God" (2 Tim. 3:16). Peter adds that human authors "*were* moved by the Holy Spirit" (2 Pet. 1:21). The pen was human; the breath was divine.

Prophecy confirms its truth: Christ's birth, betrayal, crucifixion, and resurrection were all foretold centuries before. Jesus Himself affirmed Scripture's authority, saying that "the Scripture cannot be broken" (John 10:35).

Empires have tried to destroy it, but "the word of our God stands forever" (Isa. 40:8). Its endurance and its power to transform lives prove its divine origin.

5. Is Hell Real, and Why Would a Loving God Send People There?

Key Scriptures: Matt. 25:41–46; Luke 16:19–31; 2 Thess. 1:8–9; Rom. 2:5–8; 2 Pet. 3:9

Jesus spoke about hell more than anyone else in Scripture. He described it as outer darkness, everlasting punishment, and a place of conscious separation from God.

Hell was not created for people but for the devil and his angels (Matt. 25:41). Yet those who choose to reject God share the fate of the rebellion they join. God does not force people into hell; He honors the path they persistently choose.

God's justice requires that sin be judged. But His love made a way for judgment to fall on His Son instead of on us (Isa. 53:5). Those who trust Christ escape wrath; those who reject Him remain under it (John 3:18).

Hell reveals the seriousness of sin and the magnitude of grace.

6. Aren't All Religions Basically the Same?

Key Scriptures: Acts 17:22–31; John 10:9; Eph. 2:8–9; Titus 3:5; John 19:30

Surface similarities cannot hide the core difference. Every religion teaches humanity must reach up to God. Christianity declares God reached down to us.

Religion says, "Do."

The gospel says, "Done."

Salvation is not earned by works (Eph. 2:8–9) but given by grace (Titus 3:5). Jesus did not come to start another religion; He came to end the need for them by becoming the door to salvation (John 10:9).

7. Can Science and Faith Coexist?

Key Scriptures: Col. 1:16–17; Ps. 111:2; Heb. 11:3; Rom. 1:19–20; Job 12:7–10

Science explains how creation works; Scripture explains why it exists. The two are not enemies but complementary revelations of the same truth.

Creation bears the marks of order, design, and purpose. "By Him all things were created . . . and in Him all things consist" (Col. 1:16–17). Science observes laws; Scripture reveals the Lawgiver.

Far from contradicting Scripture, scientific discovery repeatedly affirms it. The Bible spoke of the numberless stars, the paths of the seas, and the suspension of Earth long before scientific tools existed.

Science can reveal the mechanics of life, but only God gives it meaning.

Helpful Principles for Hard Conversations

Sharing truth in a skeptical world requires both courage and compassion. We are called to be "speaking truth in love"

(Eph. 4:15), which means we must care as deeply for the person as we do for the point. Here are several principles that keep our conversations Christ-like and effective:

- Listen before you answer. Proverbs 18:13 warns, "He who answers a matter before he hears *it*, it *is* folly and shame to him." Listen long enough to understand what the person actually means, not just what you think they mean. Many objections hide deep wounds such as disappointment, betrayal, or confusion. Listening reveals where healing must begin.
- Ask questions that invite reflection. Jesus often led people to truth by asking, "Who do you say that I am?" (Matt. 16:15) or "Do you believe this?" (John 11:26). Questions turn confrontations into conversations. They expose assumptions and invite people to think.
- Keep Scripture central. Arguments may stir the mind, but only the Word pierces the heart (Heb. 4:12). Let your confidence rest in what God has said, not in how clever you sound. When possible, open the Bible and let them read it for themselves. Truth seen with their own eyes carries greater weight.
- Be gentle and patient. "A servant of the Lord must not quarrel but be gentle to all, able to teach, patient, in humility correcting those who are in

opposition" (2 Tim. 2:24–25). God is often working more slowly and deeply than we realize.

- Admit when you don't know. Authenticity builds credibility. Saying "that's a good question; let me study it and get back to you" demonstrates humility and integrity, and it opens the door for a second conversation.
- Always bring it back to Jesus. Every question ultimately leads there. Whether the topic is suffering, science, or Scripture, Christ is the answer beneath them all. Don't let the discussion end at abstract ideas. Point them to the Person who embodies truth.

When tension rises, remember that you're not the Holy Spirit. Your job is to plant and water; God gives the increase (1 Cor. 3:7). Stay calm, stay prayerful, and trust that His Word will do its work long after the conversation ends.

Bringing It Together

Apologetics is not about out-arguing skeptics. It is about out-loving them with truth. The goal is never to win a debate but to bear witness to Christ. Hearts soften, not because we have outsmarted someone but because they have glimpsed grace under pressure.

We are witnesses, not prosecutors.

Truth with humility becomes an invitation.

And the Spirit uses that witness to open blind eyes.

Appendix C

KEY GOSPEL SCRIPTURES TO REMEMBER

A Clear and Simple Path for Sharing the Good News

The gospel is simple enough for a child to understand and deep enough to transform the hardest heart. These scriptures summarize the message we share—who we are, who God is, what Christ has done, how we must respond, and what God does in those who believe. Use these verses to anchor your conversations, strengthen your confidence, and point others to the hope found only in Jesus Christ.

1. The Problem of Sin – Our Need for Rescue

Romans 3:23 – *For all have sinned and fall short of the glory of God.*

- Sin is universal. Every person stands guilty before God.

Romans 3:10 – *There is none righteous, no, not one.*

- No one meets God's standard of righteousness on their own.

Isaiah 53:6 – *All we like sheep have gone astray.*

- Sin is personal rebellion; every heart wanders from God.

Isaiah 59:2 – *Your iniquities have separated you from your God.*

- Sin creates a barrier between us and God that we cannot remove.

Romans 6:23 – *For the wages of sin* is *death.*

- The consequence of sin is spiritual death and separation from God.

2. The Holiness of God – Why We Fall Short

Psalm 5:4 – *You* are *not a God who takes pleasure in wickedness.*

- God's nature is perfectly pure and cannot embrace evil.

Psalm 7:11 – *God* is *a just judge.*

- Because He is righteous, God must judge sin with justice.

1 John 1:5 – *God is light and in Him is no darkness at all.*

- God is utterly holy. He is untouched and untainted by sin.

Matthew 5:48 – *Be perfect . . . as your Father in heaven is perfect.*

- God's perfect standard reveals our complete inability to save ourselves.

3. God's Solution in Jesus Christ – The Only Sufficient Savior

John 1:1, 14 – *The Word was God. . . . And the Word became flesh.*

- Jesus is God in human flesh, the eternal Son who came to save us.

Romans 5:8 – *God demonstrates His own love toward us . . . Christ died for us.*

- Jesus died in our place because God loves sinners.

Isaiah 53:6 – *The Lord has laid on Him the iniquity of us all.*

- God placed our sin on His Son so we could be forgiven.

2 Corinthians 5:21 – *He made Him who knew no sin* to be *sin for us.*

- Jesus took our sin and gives us His righteousness in exchange.

1 Peter 2:24 – *Who Himself bore our sins in His own body on the tree.*

- Christ carried our guilt and paid our penalty through His death.

Romans 6:23 – *But the gift of God* is *eternal life in Christ Jesus our Lord.*

- Eternal life is offered as a free gift through Jesus alone.

Responding to the Gospel – Turning and Trusting

Psalm 86:5 – *You, Lord,* are *good, and ready to forgive.*

- God stands willing to forgive all who turn to Him.

Ephesians 2:8–9 – *By grace you have been saved through faith.*

- Salvation is God's gracious gift, not the result of our works.

Romans 10:13 – *Whoever calls on the name of the Lord shall be saved.*

- We are saved by believing in Christ and calling upon Him in faith.

Acts 3:19 – *Repent . . . that your sins may be blotted out.*

- God calls us to turn from sin and trust in Christ alone.

John 3:36 – *He who believes in the Son has everlasting life.*

- Belief brings life; rejection leaves a person under God's judgment.

New Life in Christ – What God Does in the Believer

John 1:12 – *As many as received Him . . . He gave the right to become children of God.*

- Through faith, God adopts us into His family.

2 Corinthians 5:17 – *If anyone* is *in Christ,* he is *a new creation.*

- Salvation produces a transformed life and a new identity.

Titus 3:5 – *He saved us through the washing of regeneration and renewing of the Holy Spirit.*

- New birth is a supernatural work of the Spirit in the believer.

Ezekiel 36:26 – *I will give you a new heart and put a new spirit within you.*

- God replaces our old heart with a new one that desires Him.

Philippians 1:6 – *He who has begun a good work in you will complete* it.

- God continues His transforming work until the day we see Christ.

These verses form the foundation of the gospel we proclaim—simple, clear, powerful, and faithful to God's Word.

Appendix D

The Essential Elements of the Gospel

Knowing What Must Be Present While Trusting the Spirit to Lead

Throughout this book, we have seen that Jesus did not rely on formulas when engaging people with the truth. He listened, discerned the heart, and spoke with wisdom and purpose. Evangelism, as modeled by Christ, is not about rehearsed presentations but about faithfully bearing witness as the Holy Spirit leads.

At the same time, the gospel is not flexible or subjective. While conversations may differ, the message we proclaim does not. This appendix is not intended to provide a script or sequence but to clarify the essential truths that define the gospel. These elements serve as theological anchors, ensuring that our witness remains faithful, even as we depend on the Spirit to apply truth to each heart.

The Essential Elements of the Gospel

1. God Is Holy and the Creator of All

The gospel begins with God, not with humanity. God is the holy Creator of all things, perfect in righteousness, just in judgment, and unchanging in His character. He is not shaped by human opinion or cultural standards. Scripture reveals Him as the rightful authority over His creation, worthy of obedience and worship.

> "Holy, holy, holy *is* the Lord of hosts" (Isa. 6:3).
> "In the beginning God created the heavens and the earth" (Gen. 1:1).

Any understanding of salvation that does not begin with the holiness and authority of God will inevitably diminish the seriousness of sin and the wonder of grace.

2. Humanity Is Sinful and Separated from God

Humanity was created in God's image, yet every person has fallen short of God's standard. Sin is not merely moral failure; it is rebellion of the heart against God's authority. Because God is holy, sin brings separation, guilt, and accountability.

> "For all have sinned and fall short of the glory of God" (Rom. 3:23).

This separation cannot be overcome by good intentions, moral improvement, or religious effort. Left to ourselves, we are unable to restore what sin has broken.

3. Jesus Christ Is the Only Savior

In love, God acted. He sent His Son, Jesus Christ, into the world. Jesus is fully God and fully man—without sin yet truly human. He lived the righteous life humanity failed to live and willingly bore the penalty of sin through His death on the cross.

> "But God demonstrates His own love toward us, in that while we were still sinners, Christ died for us" (Rom. 5:8).

On the cross, God's justice was satisfied and His mercy displayed. Sin was judged, and forgiveness was made possible, not by ignoring guilt but by bearing it through Christ's sacrifice.

4. The Resurrection Declares Christ's Victory and Authority

Jesus did not remain in the grave. He rose bodily from the dead, defeating sin and death and confirming the sufficiency of His saving work.

> "He is risen" (Matt. 28:6).

The resurrection declares more than victory. It establishes authority. The risen Christ now reigns as Lord. His resurrection assures forgiveness for those who believe and affirms that all people are ultimately accountable to Him. Salvation is not merely an invitation to admire Christ, but a call to respond to the One who lives and reigns.

5. Salvation Is by Grace Through Faith – Not Works

Salvation is not achieved through effort or earned through obedience. It is the gift of God's grace, received by faith alone.

> "For by grace you have been saved through faith . . .
> not of works" (Eph. 2:8–9).

Faith is more than intellectual agreement. It is trusting fully in Christ's finished work, turning from self-reliance, and resting in what God has done through His Son.

6. Repentance and Faith Are the Necessary Response

The gospel calls for a response. Repentance is a turning away from sin, self-rule, and false confidence. Faith is a turning toward Christ as Savior and Lord.

> "Repent therefore and be converted" (Acts 3:19).

While the Holy Spirit draws and convicts, each person is responsible to respond. The call of the gospel is gracious, but it is also serious. To hear the truth of Christ is to be confronted with a decision.

7. New Life Results in Transformation

When a person is saved, God does more than forgive the past; He gives new life. The Holy Spirit indwells the believer, bringing spiritual rebirth, new desires, and ongoing transformation.

"If anyone *is* in Christ, *he is* a new creation" (2 Cor. 5:17).

Good works do not save, but salvation produces a life that increasingly reflects Christ. Obedience flows from new life. It does not create it.

Holding Truth with Wisdom and Dependence

These elements define the gospel, but they are not always communicated in the same order or with the same emphasis. Jesus spoke truth with perfect wisdom, addressing hearts personally and purposefully. Sometimes He confronted directly; other times He invited gently. Always He spoke truth in love.

Our role is not to force conversations into a formula but to faithfully bear witness to what God has revealed, trusting the Holy Spirit to apply truth to the heart. We speak clearly, love sincerely, and depend fully on God to bring understanding and response.

- The gospel does not change.
- The conversations will.
- The Spirit remains faithful in both.

About the Author

Jason King lives in Jacksonville, Alabama, with his wife, Shelly. He is an active member of Greenbrier Road Baptist Church in Anniston, Alabama, where he serves as a Sunday school (community group) teacher. Since 2014, Jason has preached the Word weekly at the Calhoun County Jail, a work that has shaped his heart for evangelism and strengthened his desire to share Christ with those who feel far from God. He loves prayer-walking, teaching, and missions, and has served on international trips to Nicaragua, Costa Rica, and Tanzania. Jason has a passion for the gospel, a deep love for Scripture, and a desire to help believers follow Jesus' example in engaging others with truth and compassion.

www.ingramcontent.com/pod-product-compliance
Lightning Source LLC
LaVergne TN
LVHW010618100826
845148LV00014B/3014
* 9 7 8 1 6 3 2 9 6 9 9 5 8 *